A Time To Laugh... Or Cry

Part 1

An overview of the Old Testament for
preconfirmation, teen, and adult Bible study groups

by Rev. Donald F. Ginkel

What a delight it is to laugh and laugh hard. What a relief it is to cry and cry hard. *A Time To Laugh... or Cry* overviews the activity of man in the Old Testament – a time to cry because of man's stubbornness and sin and a time to laugh because of God's reaction to man's sin expressed in the Messiah. The thread of the Messiah is followed throughout. In all lessons for Part 1 and Part 2 both God and man will laugh and cry.

The questions are designed to be worked on by the class with discussion and application. Everyone should participate. All passages are from the NIV. *Students should follow the daily Bible reading which is coordinated with the history and truths of each lesson.* An excellent aid is the Concordia Self-Study Commentary.

Additional copies of this book plus other Bible studies for children and adults, confirmation, stewardship and evangelism materials may be ordered from the address below. Ask for a brochure.

+Order additional copies from
Church Press, Inc.
1-888-772-8878
info@churchpress.com
www.churchpress.com

Contents

A Time
To Laugh...
or Cry

Part 1

OLD TESTAMENT

S T U D Y

Lesson

No. 1	In the Beginning With Adam and Eve	3
No. 2	In the Garden When Everything Went Wrong	11
No. 3	At the Flood With Noah	19
No. 4	When God Made A Promise to Abraham	27
No. 5	When Abraham Faced the Supreme Test	35
No. 6	When Jacob Received the Biggest Blessing	43
No. 7	With Joseph the Slave, Prisoner, and Prime Minister	51
No. 8	When God Called Moses to Lead Israel	59
No. 9	When Israel Was Saved by the Blood of the Lamb	67
No. 10	When God Gave the Law on Sinai	73

See page 80 of this book for lesson titles for Part 2.

Scripture taken from the HOLY BIBLE: NEW INTERNATIONAL VERSION by the International Bible Society. Used by permission of Zondervan Bible Publishers.

Cover Images © 1996 PhotoDisc, Inc.

ISBN 0-9642122-4-2

Printed in the United States of America

A TIME TO LAUGH... OR CRY

In The Beginning With Adam and Eve

Genesis 1 and 2

The very first words of the Bible are: "In the beginning God created the heavens and the earth." In these 10 brief words we are plunged with magnificent suddenness into our world of space and time. An artist creates a picture and uses acrylics or oils. An engineer constructs a building and uses concrete, steel, and plastics. Just think what this says about the power, wisdom, and glory of God! For this reason alone it is right that we worship Him.

A little over six thousand years ago God made everything out of nothing. It must have been a time for Him to laugh. The first two chapters of Genesis tell how God made the world, this spinning ball we call home. This is God's account of how it happened. His Word is absolute truth. What we discover in these two chapters will come as a surprise to us, and we will laugh, too.

Opening Hymn

O Lord, my God! When I in awesome wonder
Consider all the worlds Thy hands have made.
I see the stars, I hear the rolling thunder,
Thy pow'r throughout the universe displayed.
Refrain:
Then sings my soul, my Savior God to Thee;
How great Thou art, how great Thou art!
Then sings my soul, my Savior God to Thee;
How great Thou art, how great Thou art.

When through the woods and forest glades I wander
And hear the birds sing sweetly in the trees;
When I look down from lofty mountain grandeur
And hear the brook and feel the gentle breeze: *Refrain*

Opening Prayer

We thank You, Almighty God, for the wonderful world that You made for us. Thank You for making our bodies and placing our souls inside them. Forgive us for not always appreciating our world the way we should and for the times when we do not even appreciate our own creation. Forgive us all our evil thoughts and actions through Jesus' death on the cross. Help us show our love for You by being more respectful of the earth and the environment and by showing more love to those who live around us. We give You all praise and glory for everything! In Jesus' name. Amen.

A Time To Cry or Laugh?

To emphasize their belief that God played no role in the birth of their daughter, George and Tina Rollason, of York, PA, named her Atheistic Evolution Rollason. Mr. Rollason said that his daughter's name is the couple's response to other parents' use of Biblical names. "It's kind of cute once you say it a couple of times," said Mrs. Rollason. How pathetic! The little girl may some day shed many tears over her name. And what about God? "The One enthroned in heaven *laughs*; the Lord scoffs at them" (Psalm 2:4). We believers, however, can *laugh with God* as He describes the actual beginning of our world and universe.

Genesis 1:1-2 (Read) Origin of the Universe

"In the beginning" means the beginning of time. "God" *(Elohim)* means the Almighty. "Created" is the Hebrew *bara* which means to make something out of nothing. "God's Spirit" is the Holy Spirit giving form to that which was unorganized and lifeless.

1. What existed before the creation? *nothing but God.*

2. How many persons of the Trinity were involved in the creation (1:2;1:3;1:26; John 1:1-3)? *three*

Genesis 1:3-25 (Read) Creation of the World

1. What did God make the world out of according to Hebrews 11:3?
   Faith

   How are we Christians to accept this teaching? *Faith*

2. "Day" is the Hebrew word *yom* which is a normal 24 hour period. Moses wrote for the Hebrews. With them each day began in the evening. Is it permissible to say that each day was thousands or millions of years long? Why or why not? *God used a 24 Hour Day (Yom)*

3. "According to their kinds" (Verses 21,24-26) means each according to its species.
   (a) What does this do to the various theories of evolution? *Proving of Evolution to be Wrong.*

   (b) True or (False) There can be no disagreements between what the Bible teaches and what scientists teach.

   (c) Why do you suppose that God decided to create such a variety of birds and animals? God did not create the world and everything in it to entertain Himself. He didn't give  the earth a 23-degree tilt to produce the changes of seasons for His amusement. He didn't put the moon and stars in the sky because he was bored. He did not create you for creation, but He *created creation for you.* Discuss the enormous implications of this. *for our enjoyment*

4. There are three basic beliefs concerning our world and universe:

   ● ATHEISTIC EVOLUTIONISTS deny that there is a God. They

believe that our world and universe evolved over a long period of time.

● THEISTIC EVOLUTIONISTS say that there is a Supreme Being who first made the world in its original form and that our present world developed slowly out of what was originally made. They say that each of the "days" in Genesis 1 are long periods of time, thousands or millions of years, during which the evolutionary process operated. They attempt to get the Bible to agree with the theory of evolution.

● CREATIONISTS believe that God made our world and universe and everything in it in six normal twenty-four hour periods.

We believe that all theories of evolution are contrary to God's Word. Some of the world's greatest scientists were believers in the Bible and rejected evolution: Sir Isaac Newton, Faraday, Copernicus, and many others.

Many ladies who bake a lot of apple pies have an old fashioned apple peeler. It has about ten simple parts and is very easy to assemble. You could throw those ten parts into the clothes dryer and twirl them for the next billion years, and you'd never have an apple peeler!

If it is highly improbable that something as simple as an arrowhead can be the result of chance, could a pretty rose or a singing bird come about simply by chance?

"For this is what the Lord says – He who created the heavens, He is God; He who fashioned and made the earth, He founded it; He did not create it to be empty, but formed it to be inhabited – He says: 'I am the Lord, and there is no other'" (Isaiah 45:18).

Genesis 1:26-31 (Read) Creation and Blessing of Man

1. "Us" and "Our" refer to the Persons of the Godhead: Father, Son, and Holy Spirit. "Our image, Our likeness" means that man would be created holy and be holy like God. What ultimate goal do you think God had in mind when He created man holy like Himself? _Perfect Communication, Perfect World._

2. Name two ways in which man is different from animals: _Mans has Soul. We know our maker._

3. True or False: According to verse 29, God restricted the diet of man to fruits, grains, and vegetables, and we should not eat meat (Genesis 9:3).

Genesis 2:1-3 (Read) Creation of Sabbath

All created beings in heaven and earth, including angels, had now been called into existence. The seventh day was sanctified and set aside for a holy and distinctive purpose. God rested on this day setting an example for man. The word "Sabbath" means to rest from work. The number seven is the symbol of divine operation. True or False: Verse 3 suggests that we should, even today, rest every seventh day. Why or why not? *Early Christians changed to Sunday.*

Genesis 2:4-25 (Read) Creation of Adam and Eve

1. This is a further history of the creation. "Lord" in verse 4 is the English translation of the Hebrew "Jehovah" *(Yahwey)* which means: the God of grace in His relationship with man. The vegetation is watered, not by rain from the sky (rain will come later), but by moisture that comes up from the earth. "Adam" is taken from the Hebrew word for ground *(adamah)*. Man is from the earth just like animals, but very different and superior in that God

*"But now, O Lord, Thou art our Father,
We are the clay, and Thou our potter;
And all of us are the work of Thy hand."*
ISAIAH 64:8

"breathed into his nostrils of the breath of life, and man became a living being" or possessing an immortal soul.

(a) What must we confess according to Job 33:4? _____
God made me and gives me breath

(b) What are the *benefits of appreciating* the fact that your life is a gift from God? *We have a purpose.*
Value, Gratitude, in living to honor God

(c) The feeling of worthlessness is common today, even among young people. How does the Christian have an advantage over the unbeliever in dealing with this devastating problem? ____

*Truth answer to our question come from
Creation + Calvary.*

2. "Eden" means pleasantness or delight. We often call Eden "Paradise" which is a Persian word for park. In the New Testament paradise refers to the bliss of heaven. One scholar locates Eden just north of the Euphrates and Tigris, but the actual location is not known.

3. "Tree of life and the tree of the knowledge of good and evil." These two trees received their names from the effect which the eating of their fruit would produce. The "tree of the knowledge of good and evil" was the only tree from which man was forbidden to eat. Adam and Eve had the opportunity to demonstrate their love for God through their obedience. (True) or False: The command not to eat of this tree was an opportunity, not to get man to sin, but for man to show his love for his Creator.

4. Man had "free will" (unhampered or uncoerced choice; freedom to chose) to choose between obeying or disobeying God (verses 16 and 17).

    (a) (True) or False: Among other things, Adam and Eve had the power in and of themselves to withstand any temptation to sin.

    (b) (True) or False: Since the fall into sin we no longer have "free will" and left to ourselves we can only choose to do what is evil (1 Corinthians 2:14, Ephesians 2:1).

    (c) Augustine's words on free will: "By Adam's transgression the freedom of the human will has been entirely lost. In his present corrupt state man can will and do only evil." Do you agree with his words? *yes* Why? *Man is corrupt choose evil*

5. "You will surely die" (verse 17) indicates that death is the consequence of sin and would have three aspects: (a) Immediate *spiritual death* or loss of fellowship with God, (b) *Physical death* or the separation of the soul from the body, (c) Eternal separation from God and *everlasting death* in hell. All three points touch every person today because of the Fall. Why do you suppose people fail to appreciate the terrible consequences of sin? *People don't know sin.*

6. How did Adam spend his time in the Garden of Eden? _____ *Maintain garden,*

8

7. Verses 18-25 take us back to the sixth day of creation giving us additional information. "It is not good for man to be alone" is the first negative observation the Creator makes. It is not good for man to be by himself, without companionship. Among all the animals and birds there was nothing fit for intimate companionship with Adam. "Woman" is from the Hebrew *ishah* and "man" from *ish*. Matthew Henry says, "The woman was not made out of man's head to rule over him nor out of his feet to be trampled on by him, but out of his side to be equal with him; under his arm to be protected and near his heart to be loved." What conclusions do you think Adam and Eve came to when they saw each other? _perfection made to order._

8. The Lord instituted holy matrimony by bringing Adam and Eve together.

    (a) What does Jesus tell us about marriage in Matthew 19:5-6?
    Become One and no Sepiration of marriage.

    (b) How happy do you think Adam and Eve were at the end of Chapter 2? _Pure Happiness, Content Happy to God._
    How do you think Adam and Eve felt about each other after some time went by? _Happier_
    What does this tell you about God? _Wants Good for Us._
    About holiness and marriage? _Happiness_

    (c) What are the real and underlying reasons for your unhappiness in life? _Sin_

    (d) How can you be a happier person and laugh and live more like Adam and Eve did before the fall into sin? _____
    Jewiser my life, Know where I'm going
    Does the above apply both to married *and* single people? _yes_
    Do you suppose you should share the above truths with people you know? _yes_ Why? _Might Help._

9. True or False: By your faith in Jesus as your personal Savior your

9

sins are removed from you and the holiness which Adam and Eve had is yours again.

Let's Wrap It Up

1. This lesson teaches me that God _loves me and created the world a Ahman Race, Free Will & Fellowship._

2. This lesson teaches me that Adam and Eve _were created Holy._

3. This lesson teaches me that I (truths) _Created by God bring me happiness._

    (actions) _____

_____

Closing Prayer

Closing Hymn

And when I think that God, His Son not sparing,
Sent Him to die, I scarce can take it in;
That on the cross, my burden gladly bearing,
He bled and died to take away my sin;
Refrain:
Then sings my soul, my Savior God, to Thee:
How great Thou art, how great Thou art!
Then sings my soul, my Savior God, to Thee:
How great Thou art, how great Thou art!

When Christ shall come with shout of acclamation
And take me home, what joy shall fill my heart!
Then I shall bow in humble adoration,
And there proclaim, my God, how great Thou art! *Refrain*

Bible Reading Schedule for Next Seven Days

- ❑ 1st day – Genesis 1
- ❑ 2nd day – Genesis 2
- ❑ 3rd day – Genesis 3
- ❑ 4th day – Genesis 4
- ❑ 5th day – Genesis 5
- ❑ 6th day – Genesis 6
- ❑ 7th day – Genesis 7

A TIME TO LAUGH... OR CRY

In The Garden When Everything
Went Wrong

Genesis 3 – 4:1

A young girl was trudging along a mountain path, trying to reach her grandmother's house. It was bitter cold. Suddenly she heard a rustle at her feet. Looking down, she saw a snake. Before she could move, the snake spoke to her. He said, "I am about to die. It is too cold for me up here, and I am freezing. There is no food around, and I am starving. Please let me under your coat, and take me with you."

"No," replied the girl. "I know your kind. You are a rattlesnake. If I pick you up, you will bite me, and your bite is poisonous." "No, no," replied the snake. "If you help me, you will be my best friend. I will treat you differently."

The little girl sat down on a rock for a moment to rest and think things over. She looked at the beautiful markings on the snake and had to admit that it was the most beautiful snake she had ever seen. Suddenly, she said, "I believe you. I will save you. All living things deserve to be treated with kindness."

She reached over, put the snake gently under her coat and proceeded toward her grandmother's house.

Within a moment, she felt a sharp pain in her side. The snake had bitten her. "How could you do this to me?" she cried. "You promised that you would not bite me, and I trusted you!" "You knew what I was when you picked me up," hissed the snake as he slithered away.

This parable sets the stage for the true story of Adam and Eve who trusted a snake in the Garden of Eden. When it was over, they cried. God cried. It was the darkest day the world has ever seen. And today we cry, too!

Opening Hymn (Tune: "The Happy Wanderer")

A joyful noise unto our God Who made the land and sea;
He framed them both with all their host, Created you and me.
Clap your hands, shout for joy, bless His name;
Sing the praise of God your Maker.
When He spoke, it was done – Creation by His Word.

The sparrow and leviathan Are fed by God's own hand;
The cattle on a thousand hills Exist by His command.
Clap your hands, shout for joy, bless His name;
Sing the praise of God our Keeper:
He provides, He protects, Upholds us by His word.

Opening Prayer

Heavenly Father, help us understand what really happened on the saddest day in history, the day God and Adam and Eve cried. Like our first parents, we have made some bad choices. We have purposely permitted Satan to tempt us. We have listened to his lies. Please forgive us. Show us the great love You have for us in sending Jesus to save us from Satan and sin. Help us obey You and not the Devil. Father, bless us in this study that we may laugh again, here and in heaven. Amen.

Something Wrong

Not long ago Mary Sams, 27, got out of jail on probation and child-support violations. She immediately looked up her old boyfriend, Fred

Hoyer, in the Chicago, IL, liquor store where he worked and tried to persuade him to resume the relationship. According to police, Sams – who outweighs Hoyer by 40 pounds – threw him onto a truck ramp in the back of the store, broke 23 liquor bottles, wrapped him in an apron, and sat on him for more than two hours until he agreed to reconcile. One could say that things were not going well for Mr. Narr that day. But of all the sad days men have experienced, none will compare in scope to what happened in the Garden of Eden on the day when *everything* went wrong.

Genesis 3:1-7 (Read) The Temptation and Fall

1. Suddenly and very unexpectedly trouble came to Paradise. The serpent was a most cunning and beautiful animal having legs. Satan entered this animal for the temptation. Satan's fall in heaven preceded the fall in the Garden. What do Isaiah 14:12-24 and

   Revelation 12:9 tell us? _____

   _____

   Satan is an expert in seduction. He suggested that Eve must have misunderstood God's command. His question was: "Eve, is it possible that a Being as good as God could really have said you cannot eat of any tree?" He includes all trees.

2. Eve's reply was good. She corrected the distortion. Then she added these words to what God had originally said: "You must not touch it." This is the first indication of a small amount of bitterness toward God. At this point Eve is starting to fail. She suggests that if she touches it she will die, thereby ascribing more danger to the tree than to the real peril which was disobeying God. Satan is quick to notice. He continues the attack.

   (a) "You will not surely die." What does John 8:44 say? _____

   _____

   (b) Satan assures Eve that no harm will come and holds out the assurance of valuable benefits from eating the forbidden fruit.

   What two things did Satan say would happen if she ate? ____

   _____

   What would her eyes be opened to? _____

What is untrue about Satan's promise (verses 4-5) _____

_____

What is true? _____

What was Satan's immediate goal with Eve? _____

Long range goal? _____

Does he still have these goals today? _____

(c) Eve saw that the fruit was to be desired. What does James 1:15

say? _____ James 1:13-14 adds

these truths: _____

(d) How does our sin differ from Eve's sin? _____

3. The appeal was threefold: (a) good for food, (b) pleasing to the eye, (c) desirable for gaining wisdom. These words summarize every temptation and sin. Eve takes of the fruit, and sin takes Eve captive. The sinner seeks company and seduces others. Adam joins her in sin. The choice was between God (Who always tells the truth) and Satan (who never tells the truth), and they chose Satan.

(a) True or False: We also have to choose between the devil and God on a daily basis.

(b) What does Satan use to tempt us to sin today? _____

(c) How can we be successful when we are tempted (1 Peter 5:8-9)?

_____

4. Their eyes were opened not only to sin, but that which comes with sin: guilt, shame, sorrow. In their embarrassment they sewed fig leaves together. Even though they were husband and wife they were ashamed of their nakedness. They would rather cover themselves than confess.

Genesis 3:8-13 (Read) The Investigation

1. God spoke as He walked in the Garden making His presence known to Adam and Eve, but they hid themselves. The Lord God called to Adam, "Where are you?" How gracious He was to the first sinners. He was beginning to work out redemption rather than simple condemnation. This is signified by His covenant or redemptive name, "Jehovah" *(Yahweh)*, rather than His creative

name, "God" (Elohim). The infinite God reveals Himself redemptively to finite man.

(a) Man was afraid after he sinned. What could he not enjoy anymore? _____

(b) True or False: God must carry out His threat to punish sin.

(c) True or False: After man sinned, God would have been justified in turning His back on them and leaving them to their fate.

(d) According to 2 Peter 2:4 "God _____

angels when they _____, but sent them to

_____, putting them into _____

to be held for _____ "

2. Adam replied, "I was afraid... I was naked; so I hid." This is the plight of every sinner in the presence of a holy God. God continues the questioning to bring Adam to an admission of his guilt. "Have you eaten from the tree...?" Pressed and cornered, Adam makes only a partial admission of wrongdoing. Yes he ate of the tree, but he places the blame on the woman. Adam even dared to put the blame for his sin upon God Himself! "The woman *You* gave me." We are not surprised that God doesn't even respond to Adam. His words are too foolish to merit a response. When God asked Eve what she had done she replied, "The serpent deceived me." The Hebrew verb for "deceive" is to seduce or trick into temptation. She admits guilt, but passes off the blame.

(a) Why should we not try to escape our admission of sin by lying or blaming others? _____

(b) Eve said, "The Devil made me do it!" What are some excuses that we offer today? _____

_____

Why are these foolish excuses? _____

Genesis 3:14 (Read) Satan Cursed

From what was one of the most beautiful and intelligent animals in the Garden, the serpent is now lowered to a despicable crawling reptile which we loath to this day. This is a picture of the greater punishment waiting all the evil angels and their followers when they are punished in eternal hellfire. True or False: The sight of a snake should remind us of the effects of sin in the Garden.

Genesis 3:15 (Read) The Promise of Redemption

This is the first announcement of the coming Messiah, Jesus Christ. Eve's offspring or "seed" is singular, a reference to the God-Man, Jesus. God is speaking to Satan and Adam and Eve. Enmity means hostility, conflict, or warfare which would come to a culmination in a tremendous battle on Calvary. "He will crush your head" refers to the death blow that the Messiah will inflict on Satan on the cross. "You will bruise His heel" says that in this battle for the souls of men, the Messiah will suffer mortal wounds. Both parties will be wounded, but Satan's wound will be eternally fatal.

Genesis 3:16-24 (Read) Man and Earth Cursed

1. God would forgive Adam and Eve their sin and receive them back into His family, but they would have to endure the consequences of their sin in this world. For the woman pregnancy and birth would be accompanied by severe pain. She would be dependent upon her husband and be in submission to him, and he would exercise authority over her. God then curses the ground and promises that by strenuous labor man would make his living. The final penalty comes the day they physically die and their bodies return to dust. It is truly time for God and man to cry.

    (a) How would you answer someone who says, "This curse is not fair!"? *It is Just*

    (b) Read Romans 5:12. What effect did Adam and Eve's sin have on all men? *Sin came to everyone & death.*
    What is original sin? *Born with it.*
    Read Romans 5:18. What is the "one act of righteousness"? *Christ death on the cross,*
    What two things does it bring? *Eternal life & Justification*
    How do you get them (Romans 5:1)? *Faith alone through faith*

2. "Eve" means life. In the face of the judgment of death pronounced by God, Adam indicates that he believes the promise of life will

16

come from the Seed or Descendant of Eve. God tempers His justice with mercy, and Adam quickly responds – so should we! Why do you think most people do not respond to God's mercy? _They feel they do not sin._
What can we do to help them? _Pray + be example_

3. What does verse 21 show about God? _Provides for our need_
We, too, need to be clothed – in the holiness of Jesus. Nicolaus L. von Zinzendorf wrote:
Jesus, Your blood and righteousness My beauty are, my glorious dress; Mid flaming worlds, in these arrayed, with joy shall I lift up my head.

4. So that man would not eat of the tree of life and perpetuate his sad existence on earth, God drove him from the Garden. This was as much an act of God's mercy as it was His justice. We lost our "rose garden," but a better one is coming! God drove man out. This suggests that man may have resisted his expulsion. Cherubim are posted at the entrance to prevent reentry. Not a time to laugh.

Genesis 4:1 (Read) The Redeemer?

There is good reason to believe that Eve thought her first child was the promised Savior (3:15). Her literal exclamation: "I have the man, the Lord." (*Yehwey* – God of grace). Luther gives this translation: "I have the man, the Lord." She seems to have believed that God's promise of the Messiah in 3:15 was fulfilled in this child. We know that this son was not the Savior. In fact, he became a murderer when he killed his brother. Eve had to believe in a future event to be saved (As did a host of others mentioned in Hebrews 11). We believe in a past event. Through Jesus' suffering and death upon the cross there is forgiveness for all our sin, the start of a new life here and a perfect life with God forever in heaven (Paradise restored, only better). And it's a free gift from God by faith in Jesus. Now we can *laugh* – and we should!

Let's Wrap It Up

1. This lesson teaches me that God _forgiving God Savior for the human race + Death to Satan_

2. This lesson teaches me that Satan _enemy a our enemy._

17

3. This lesson teaches me that Adam and Eve _rather listen to the devil then God who loves them without preconditions._

4. This lesson teaches me that I (truths) _need to daily believe God loves me._

(actions) _believe God + Son as my Savior and follow him daily, ask for strainght_

Closing Prayer

Closing Hymn (Tune: "The Happy Wanderer")

Sing your praise to our Savior, God And also born true Man;
The Word made flesh, made under law, Removed law's curse and ban.
Clap your hands, shout for joy, bless His name;
Sing praise for Christ our Master:
Crucified, Jesus died, He bought us with a price.

Behold, the Sun of Righteousness With healing in His wings,
Took on Himself a servant's form, Removed death's dreadful sting.
Clap your hands, shout for joy, bless His name;
Sing the praise of Christ our Savior:
Once He died, now He lives Our Advocate with God.

To God the Father, Spirit, Son Be honor, glory, praise,
Which was and is and is to come, At closing of our days.
Clap your hands, shout for joy, bless His name;
Sing the praise of God forever!
Bless the Lord, O my soul, with joyful lips. Amen!

Bible Reading Schedule for the Next Seven Days

❑ 1st day – Genesis 8   ❑ 5th day – Genesis 12
❑ 2nd day – Genesis 9   ❑ 6th day – Genesis 13
❑ 3rd day – Genesis 10   ❑ 7th day – Genesis 14
❑ 4th day – Genesis 11

Lesson 3

A TIME TO LAUGH... OR CRY

At The Flood With Noah

Genesis 6:1-10,13-22; 7; 8; 9:12-17

The human race spread throughout the earth, but it became very wicked. Mankind was obsessed with evil. Violence was everywhere. It was time to cry. For 120 years God tried to convince men to stop their wickedness, but the people refused. In His grief, God decided to destroy all people and animals, and He would do so by sending a flood. Only Noah found favor with God; he and his family would be spared. Noah was a man of faith. In obedience to God's command he built an ark. Noah, his family, and the animals entered the ark. God Himself shut the door. For seven days nothing happened. Then the flood came. One year later the ark came to rest. Now it was time to laugh. Noah thanked God with special sacrifices. God said that He would never again destroy mankind in a flood. The promise of the Messiah remained intact, and that's why *we* can laugh.

Opening Hymn

Rock of Ages, cleft for me, Let me hide myself in Thee;
Let the water and the blood From Thy riven side which flowed
Be of sin the double cure, Cleanse me from its guilt and pow'r.

Not the labors of my hands Can fulfil Thy Law's demands;
Could my zeal no respite know, Could my tears forever flow,
All for sin could not atone; Thou must save, and Thou alone.

Opening Prayer

Almighty God, help us understand the
implications of Noah, the flood, and the
rainbow. Surely You are a God who will not
tolerate sin. We confess that many times we
have thought too lightly of sin. Like the people
in Noah's day we are sometimes slow to believe
You. Please forgive us. As Noah was thankful for the ark so we are
thankful for the protection You provide us, especially the protection of
the forgiveness of all our sins through the blood of Jesus. Give us
special insights as we proceed in this Bible study, and we will give You
the glory and praise for the good things that come from it in our lives.
Hear us for the sake of Jesus, our dear Savior. Amen.

How Bad Was it?

Accused murderer Bob Russell Williams Jr., allegedly telling a
Bakersfield, CA, police officer that he did not deserve the death penalty
(which could be given if the murder occurred in conjunction with other
felonies): "I might have killed that lady, but I'm no burglar." That is
the kind of mentality that was prevalent in Noah's day. How bad was
it? Let's see.

Genesis 6:1-10 Coming Judgment

1. In fifteen hundred years the numbers and wickedness of man
    exploded. Men of the tribe of Seth picked wives from the ungodly
    Cainite for pure sensual reasons. God finally gave men one
    hundred and twenty years of grace. God's Word was preached to
    them. 2 Peter 2:5 says, "God did not spare the ancient world when
    He brought the flood on its ungodly people, but protected Noah, a
    preacher of righteousness, and seven others." Noah was God's

preacher, but his preaching had no effect. Every thought of the heart of man was wicked continually. Some of the saddest words in the Bible are found in verse 6. God concluded, "I am grieved that I have made them (man)." With sorrowful words God said He would destroy all people who persist in their wickedness. The verb *maha* (verse 7) means "to rub over or wipe away," signifying that God was going to wipe man off the face of the earth.

(a) What were people like at this time? Jesus tells us: "As it was in the days of Noah, so it will be at the coming of the Son of Man. For in the days before the flood, people were eating and drinking, marrying and giving in marriage, up to the day Noah entered the ark; and they knew nothing about what would happen until the flood came and took them all away. That is how it will be at the coming of the Son of Man" (Matthew 24:37-39).

In a few words, what were people like? *Sinful, no love for God.*

What warning is there for us? *Honor God and give him 1st place in our lives*

What do most people seem to be occupied with today? *pleasures of the world* The first destruction was by *water* The final destruction will be by *fire*.

(b) Noah didn't seem to mind that people thought he was foolish by believing and trusting in the one true God while we seem to mind a great deal if it happens to us (Example: Saying a mealtime prayer in a restaurant or sharing the Good News of Jesus with a friend). What encouragement can we get from Noah on this? *God 1st in his life.*

2. Only Noah and his family would be spared. How was this possible according to Hebrews 11:7? *Save by his faith not by his work.*

Noah's life was outward evidence of the faith in his heart. What does your life show about your faith? *Practice it more openly. Afraid to be different.*

3. Noah found favor or grace in the eyes of the Lord. The Messianic line would run through him, and finally the Savior would come. This is the first mention of "grace" in the Bible. When Noah found grace, what did he find (Definition of the word)? *Undeserve*
   Love for him as the Messiah

4. Noah was a "righteous man" because of his faith in the promises of God's grace which would ultimately provide a Redeemer. (True) or False: Noah believed in the same Savior we believe in in order to be saved.

Genesis 6:13-22 Instructions on Ark

1. Man and the earth in the form it had then would be destroyed. Things would never be the same. Two of the consequences of this destruction would be that the soil would lose much of its power to produce food and the age span of man would significantly decrease. All this should be a warning to us today that God will not permit man to simply continue on in uninterrupted unbelief and sin. As destruction came then, so history will repeat itself in a second and total destruction of the world. What effect should this Bible truth have on your emotions and daily living? _____

   _____

2. What are the dimensions of the ark? _____

   It was especially well designed to ride out a world-wide flood. "Ark" means box. "Nave" means ship, another word for our sanctuary or church. The ark is a type or picture of Christ and His holy Church.

   (a) What do insurance companies usually call floods, earthquakes, tornadoes, etc? _____

   _____ Are they? _____

   (b) True or False: The Church of Jesus Christ will be the only safe place to be when fire destruction comes on Judgment Day.

3. "Floodwaters" (verse 7) comes from the Hebrew *mabbul* which means deluge or catastrophic flood. Luther calls the flood a *sintflood* (sin flood) because it comes as a direct result of man's sin.

4. Why, specifically, was Noah's task mammoth? _____

_____

5. Read verse 22. How come? _____

Genesis 7 The Flood

1. Of what significance to us should the repeated statement be that Noah did *exactly* what God had commanded him (verse 5)? _____

_____

2. Why should we follow his example? _____

3. One time a church secretary handed her pastor a card. On one side it said: "Question! Who was the greatest financier in the Bible?" On the other side it read: "Answer: Noah – his stock was afloat when every else's was being liquidated!" A great pun, but also a great truth.

4. With Noah, his family, and the animals safe in the ark the cataclysm began, 1,656 years after the creation. "The springs of the great deep burst forth" and the "floodgates of the heavens were opened" (verse 11). Extra large amounts of underground water were permitted to break loose, and large amounts of water held high in the sky were permitted to come down to produce the flood. It is believed that the pre-flood earth had a warm temperature all over, but this would radically change after the flood so that cold and heat and seasons would begin (8:22). It rained for forty days and may have continued for a long period after that. The entire earth was covered with water including the highest mountain. Every living thing died. Geological formations and fossil remains found all over the world indicate a universal flood. Who can picture the terror that must have been present as man and animals tried in vain to escape the water?

5. True or False: It was too late for people to repent and escape death once the flood began.

6. The Apostle Peter writes in 1 Peter 3:19-21: "Jesus went and preached to the spirits in prison (hell) who disobeyed long ago when God waited patiently in the days of Noah while the ark was being built. In it only a few people, eight in all, were saved through water, and this water symbolizes baptism that now saves you also -- not the removal of dirt from the body but the pledge of a good

conscience toward God. It saves you by the resurrection of Jesus Christ." What saved Noah from destruction? _____ _____ What will save us from eternal destruction? _____

7. 2 Peter 3:6-7,12 says, "By these waters also the world of that time was deluged and destroyed. By the same word the present heavens and earth are reserved for fire, being kept for the day of judgment and destruction of ungodly men... That day will bring about the destruction of the heavens by fire, and the elements will melt in the heat." How does God's destruction of mankind at the time of the flood differ from His destruction of mankind on the Last Day?

    _____

8. The ark points to a place of safety for us. What is it (the word "nave" might be a clue)? _____

    _____

Genesis 8 End of Flood

Noah and his family were in the ark for a year and ten days. After five months the flood was at its peak. Gradually the waters receded. Noah could see mountains coming out of the water. Finally, the ark came to rest on the mountains of Ararat in Armenia. From a number of documentary films and books it appears that the remains of the ark have been discovered there. Noah waited very patiently in the Ark for

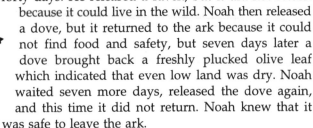 forty days. He released a raven, but it did not return because it could live in the wild. Noah then released a dove, but it returned to the ark because it could not find food and safety, but seven days later a dove brought back a freshly plucked olive leaf which indicated that even low land was dry. Noah waited seven more days, released the dove again, and this time it did not return. Noah knew that it was safe to leave the ark.

Noah and his family now embarked on a totally new beginning. His first act was to build an altar and sacrifice a burnt offering as did all of God's people throughout Old Testament history. The sacrifice pointed forward to Christ who would offer Himself on the cross as a sacrifice for our sins. God promised that He would never again repeat this kind of judgment. Verse 22 speaks of the changes on earth, extremes of heat and cold, distinct seasons, and a change in the way the earth will produce food. In what words is original sin taught in verse 21? _____

Genesis 9:12-17 The Covenant

1. God promises man and beast that there will be no repeat of the flood with the sign of the rainbow.

    (a) True or False: Man did not have anything to contribute that would encourage God to enter into this covenant. It was totally an agreement coming from His grace.

    (b) This illustrates the greater mercy to come, the mercy of Jesus nailed to the Cross for the sins of all men. What did we have to contribute to God's gift of Jesus and His suffering and death

    for our sins? _____
    Isaac Watts writes –

    > *Alas! and did my Savior bleed, And did my Sov'reign die?*
    > *Would He devote that sacred head For sinners such as I?*

    > *Was it for sins that I had done He groaned upon the tree?*
    > *Amazing pity, grace unknown, And love beyond degree!*

2. We tend to excuse the sinner and his sin. Many people and churches say we need to understand why the sinner is the way he is – his parents, his environment, etc. How does the story of the flood deal with the subject of sin (Consider it in the light of God's

    justice and then His grace)? _____

3. As we follow the genealogies in Genesis we notice man's life shrinking fast. True or False: The reduction of life span on earth is more an act of God's grace than His judgment. In either case, why?

4. True or False: When man sins and follows his own will, he must either receive God's forgiveness or else go on in his sin and receive punishment.

5. True or False: It is one thing for man to sin and then come back to

God and ask for His forgiveness; it is another thing for man to sin and not really care.

Let's Wrap It Up

1. This story teaches me that God _____

   _____

2. This story teaches me that Noah _____

   _____

3. This story teaches me that I (truths) _____

   _____

   (actions) _____

   _____

Closing Prayer

Closing Hymn

Nothing in my hand I bring; Simply to Thy cross I cling.
Naked, come to Thee for dress; Helpless, look to Thee for grace;
Foul, I go the fountain fly; Wash me, Savior, or I die.

While I draw this fleeting breath, When mine eyelids close in death,
When I soar to worlds unknown, See Thee on Thy judgment throne,
Rock of Ages, cleft for me, Let me hide myself in Thee.

Bible Reading Schedule for the Next Seven Days

- ❑ 1st day – Genesis 15
- ❑ 2nd day – Genesis 16
- ❑ 3rd day – Genesis 17
- ❑ 4th day – Genesis 18
- ❑ 5th day – Genesis 19
- ❑ 6th day – Genesis 20
- ❑ 7th day – Genesis 21

Lesson 4

A TIME TO LAUGH... OR CRY

When God Made A Promise To Abraham

Genesis 12:1-7; 13:1-13; 15:1-6,12-16; 17:3-16

Imagine that you lived in a nice home with your family. You're comfortable and happy. You have beautiful clothes and enough money to do most anything you wish. Suddenly God's voice breaks the tranquility by telling you to pack a few things and, with your family, move. When you ask, "Where to?", God answers, "I'll let you know later. It's a very nice place. I will give you an abundance of physical and spiritual gifts, but on your way you'll have to live in a tent." What would you do? Would you obey God or disobey? A man named Abraham once had a similar choice to make. Let's see how God kept His promise to Abraham. It was a time to laugh. And since what happened involves you in a *very, very big way*, you'll laugh, too, in fact, forever!

Opening Hymn

I am weak but Thou art strong; Jesus, keep me from all wrong;
I'll be satisfied as long As I walk, let me walk close to Thee.
Refrain: Just a closer walk with Thee, Grant it, Jesus, is my plea,
    Daily walking close to Thee, Let it be, dear Lord, let it be.

Through this world of toil and snares, If I falter, Lord, who cares?
Who with me my burden shares? None but Thee, dear Lord, none but
Thee. *Refrain*

Opening Prayer

Heavenly Father, we look forward to this Bible study, a time to
laugh when You made a beautiful promise to Abraham. Father, so often
we are weak and afraid. We have not always trusted You. Give to us
the same kind of faith that You gave Abraham. We thank You for
making us Your children. We thank You that heaven is our home. As
we travel through life, help us believe every one of Your promises.
Bless us now as we study, share, and grow. We pray in Jesus' name.
Amen.

A Time To Say "Yes"

6-year old Jon Kecks was giving the dentist a hard time. He
wouldn't open his mouth. "Come on, Jon," coaxed Dr. John Donohue,
"I'm not going to giving you a shot today." Through clenched teeth Jon
replied, "And you're not going to look in my mouth either." Ah, we
understand Jon's feelings. But sometimes, in situations like this, it is
wise to say "Yes." Case in point – Abraham. Because he said yes we
can laugh today, and we'll laugh forever! One song (to the tune of
"When the Saints" says –

We got our call, we got our call, We got our call in Abraham;
We made a covenant through Moses, And He's coming back again!

Genesis 12:1-7 The Call of Abram

The time was 2,000 B.C. Abram and his family lived in Ur of the
Chaldees. Ur was an ancient city situated on the Euphrates River. Many
different races of people lived there, and many heathen religions were
practiced.

Abram moved to Haran which was several hundred miles

northwest of Ur. At Haran God told Abram, "Leave your country... and go to a land I will show you." That land is Canaan. Later it would be called the Promised Land. Today it is called Palestine. It's a strip of plains, mountains, and valleys 150 miles long and 50 miles wide.

God promised to make a great nation come from Abram and that would be Israel which would come into being in the land of Egypt. All of this would lead to the greatest gift of all promised in verses 2 and 3. Israel would be the channel through which the Savior would be born. Through Abram, then, every person on earth would be blessed.

1. Initially Abram was in the wrong country. In what sense are you "living in the wrong country"? _____

2. By what other names has the land of Canaan been known? _____

3. Use just one word to describe how Abram was to show his faith in God: _____

4. Many times Abram stopped and built an altar. What do we mean by the "family altar"? _____

Genesis 13:1-13 Choices

In his journey to Egypt Abram made some mistakes, big ones. On his return to Canaan he was a new man with remarkable faith and godly virtues and an abundance of wealth. Lot, who had been traveling with Abram, also had large flocks and herds. To avoid conflict between the herdsmen of the two men, Abram made a generous offer to Lot: Lot should choose first that part of the country that he would claim for himself. Abram was satisfied with what was left. Lot was selfish and greedy. He picked the most fertile part of the country, the lower valley, where he hoped to have greater opportunity for prosperity. Here the wicked cities of Sodom and Gomorrah were situated. First he moved his family close to Sodom and then into the city. Chapters 18 and 19 reveal how horrible the mistake was.

1. What honorable traits did Abram reveal in giving Lot first choice? _____

2. Was he wise or foolish in giving Lot first choice? _____

3. One morning, at 2:55 a.m., a 20-year-old Olathe, KS, man hopped over a fence and into a yard... containing three Rottweilers and a German shepherd. The intruder ended up being taken to the hospital with dog bites over most of his body. Police Lt. Vernon Watson said, "Here we have someone who was in a place where he shouldn't have been. He definitely picked the wrong yard." Lot was just as foolish. He was foolish in two ways. First, he was selfish with regard to the land. Second, he chose to take up residence in a very wicked city. What do bad decisions, like these two, bring us

when we make them? _____

_____

Genesis 15:1-6,12-16 God's Promise with Abram

Abram, despite his many victories, was despondent. The burning question for him was, "God, what can you give me since I go childless?"

1. In verse 1 God gave two reasons why Abram

   should not despair; they are: _____

_____

2. What do those two points mean? _____

_____

3. Why do these two points also apply to you? _____

_____

A mere servant would be his heir without a child of his own. Now God states explicitly that not Eliezer but Abram's own son would be heir. Abram would be 100 years old and Sarai 90. God takes him outside and shows him the star-studded sky, promising Abram an innumerable spiritual family as well as a large physical family. We believers are members of Abram's spiritual family just like the folk song says:

Father Abraham had many sons, Many sons had father Abraham.
I am one of them and so are you, So lets just praise the Lord!

Read verse 6 again. Abram's faith was a saving faith because its object was the coming Savior, Jesus Christ. He not only believed the promise in general, but he accepted salvation through faith, the same faith mentioned in Romans 3:25-26:

"God presented Jesus as a sacrifice of atonement, through faith in His blood. He did this to demonstrate His justice, because in His forbearance He had left the sins committed beforehand unpunished – He did it to demonstrate His justice at the present time, so as to be just and the one who justifies those who have faith in Jesus."

Think of it – Abram was declared righteous, holy, soley on the basis of his faith in the divine promise of the Savior! How can we be sure of that? Romans 4:18-25 reads:

"Against all hope, Abraham in hope believed and so became the father of many nations, just as it had been said to him, 'So shall your offspring be.' Without weakening in his faith, he faced the fact that his body was as good as dead – since he was about a hundred years old – and that Sarah's womb was also dead. Yet he did not waver through unbelief regarding the promise of God, but was strengthened in his faith and gave glory to God, being fully persuaded that God had power to do what he had promised. This is why 'it was credited to him as righteousness.' The words 'it was credited to him' were written not for him alone, but also for us, to whom God will credit righteousness – for us who believe in Him who raised Jesus our Lord from the dead. He was delivered over to death for our sins and was raised to life for our justification."

1. What is the thrust of these verses as they relate to Abram? _____

   _____

   Who are these words for? _____

2. Read Genesis 15:6 again. What does it mean that you are now justified? _____

   Should this make you laugh? _____ How hard? _____

   For how long? _____

Abram literally took God at His Word; we need to do the same. In Genesis 15:12-16 God reveals the journey to Egypt where Abram's people would be in slavery and bondage for a little more than 400 years. His people entered Egypt 1,870 B.C. The Exodus began about 1,440 B.C. Abram would die in old age and in peace.

Genesis 17:3-16 The Promise Renewed

1. Abram now becomes Abraham, which, in Hebrew, means, "father of a multitude." God renews the promise of the Messiah, including the promise of Canaan. As the rainbow was to be a sign of God's love, so circumcision would be a physical mark on the flesh as a sign of God's love and grace. All males of the chosen race would be circumcised eight days after birth. Whoever was not circumcised would have no part in this covenant. Circumcision has been replaced by baptism in the New Testament. Colossians 2:11-12:

   > "In Him (Jesus) you were also circumcised, in the putting off of the sinful nature, not with a circumcision done by the hands of men but with the circumcision done by Christ, having been buried with Him in baptism and raised with Him through your faith in the power of God, who raised Him from the dead."

2. Sarai is changed to Sarah which means princess. Those who came from her would have a royal lineage: King David, and, finally, the King of kings, the Lord Jesus Christ would come from her. Matthew 1:1-2 begins the most important geneology of them all:

   > "A record of the genealogy of Jesus Christ the son of David, the son of Abraham: Abraham was the father of Isaac, Isaac the father of Jacob, Jacob the father of Judah and his brothers..."

   Sarah could laugh, too, because of the Messiah. How happy was she? Her son's name, "Isaac," means "laughter." She lived to be 127 years old.

3. Hebrews 11:1 says: "Now faith is being sure of what we hope for and certain of what we do not see."

   How do you demonstrate your faith? _____

   _____

4. Divide your class into four group; each group take one verse and write down the blessing promised you:

   (a) John 3:16 _____

   (b) 1 John 1: 9 _____

   (c) John 14:27 _____

   (d) Romans 8:38-39 _____

5. Israel became God's chosen people. Why did God choose them?

_____

We are God's chosen people headed for the real Promised Land. Why did God choose us? _____

6. Let's take a closer look at our faith.

(a) What place do doubts and fears have in our faith today? _____

(b) What promises of God do you sometimes doubt? _____

(c) Is it possible to have saving faith without doubt? _____

My Faith Looks Up to Thee

Let's Wrap It Up

1. This story teaches me that God _____

_____

2. This story teaches me that Abraham _____

_____

3. This story teaches me that (truths) _____

_____

(actions) _____

_____

Closing Prayer

Closing Hymn

Lord, take my hand and lead me Upon life's way;
Direct, protect, and feed me From day to day.
Without Your grace and favor I go astray;
So take my hand, O Savior, And lead the way.

Lord, when the tempest rages, I need not fear;
For You, the Rock of Ages, Are always near.

Close by Your side abiding, I fear no foe,
For when Your hand is guiding, In peace I go.

Lord, when the shadows lengthen And night is come,
I know that You will strengthen My steps toward home,
And nothing can impede me, O blessed Friend!
So, take my hand and lead me Unto the end.

Bible Reading Schedule for the Next Seven Days

❑ 1st day – Genesis 22
❑ 2nd day – Genesis 23
❑ 3rd day – Genesis 24
❑ 4th day – Genesis 25
❑ 5th day – Genesis 26
❑ 6th day – Genesis 27
❑ 7th day – Genesis 28

Lesson 5

A TIME TO LAUGH... OR CRY

When Abraham Faced
The Supreme Test

Genesis 22:1-19

If you had been Mrs. Joan Meyer, what would you have done? She faced a seemingly impossible decision. One daughter was lost beneath the waters of a pond near their home. Another daughter whom Joan had pulled from the pond was lying motionless on the ground. Her screams for help had not been heard. She gave CPR to daughter Susan, 7 years old. Soon the girl began to respond. Time to laugh. Firemen later recovered the body of daughter Pamela, 3 years old. Time to cry. A man named Abraham had a similar decision to make with greater implications affecting his only son and awesome implications affecting you today and for eternity!

Opening Hymn

On a hill far away stood an old rugged cross,
The emblem of suffering and shame;
And I love that old cross where the dearest and best
For a world of lost sinners was slain.
Chorus:
So I'll cherish the old rugged cross,
'Til my trophies at last I lay down;
I will cling to the old rugged cross,
And exchange it some day for a crown.

O that old rugged cross, so despised by the world,
Has a wondrous attraction for me;
For the dear Lamb of God left His glory above
To bear it to dark Calvary. *Chorus:*

Opening Prayer

Dear Father God, like Abraham You had only one Son. Like Abraham You loved Him intensely. And like Abraham You were willing to sacrifice that beloved Son so that we might be spared eternal death and live with You in heaven some day. Father, it must have hurt You deeply when, in Your justice, You placed Your wrath over our sins upon Your Son on the cross. Surely it was a time for You to weep. Help us better understand the decision You had to make – in order to save us You had to sacrifice the most precious Person to You. Forgive us our sins because of that death. Give us whatever tests we need to make You number one in life and death, so that we can laugh with You forever. We pray in Jesus' name. Amen.

Putting God First

A girl named Mary tells what happened to her mother under Communism in the old Soviet Union. She was put on trial for being a Christian and found guilty. Her children were then placed in the courtroom, and the prosecutor shouted at her: "Whom do you love more, your own children or your idol, this Jesus? You are a mother. There are your children. Deny God and you may go home with them – or else you'll never see them again. We'll kill you." The Christian mother sat there with her scarf covering her eyes and said, "God sees everything. I will be faithful to God. He will reward me accordingly." As they led her away the children, including Mary, cried to her, "Mother, do not leave us," she did not even turn to them. She met this severe test of her faith.

Genesis 22:1-2 The Test

Who or what is number one in our lives? Sometimes we make things number one, but that often brings disappointment. If we make another human being number one in life, we are bound to be disappointed because people always let us down. The same is true of wealth and fame. In Genesis 22 God is demonstrating that He must be first and, if He is, we will never be disappointed.

Abraham's faith had been severely tested as he waited for a son. Through his son God would make Israel a great nation. Through this son the Savior of the world would come. At the time of this text Isaac was 15 to 20 years old. He was as dear to his father as any child could be, but more so here because of the coming Messiah. All the hopes and dreams of Abraham and all our hopes and dreams were, at this point, centered on Isaac. God could not have given Abraham a more difficult test.

"Abraham, how much do you love Me? How much are you willing to give to Me? How much? Your son? I don't want any of your thousands of animals, nor your land, nor your fine linen or gold or silver or jewels. I want your most prized possession. I want your own son that you've waited for for 100 years. He is a brilliant young man, and you have grown to love him so much. I want you to give him to Me on an altar."

1. "Your only son" (*yahid*), "the unique one, the one and only son." In what two ways was Isaac unique? _____

    _____

    Isaac was a type of Christ. How was He unique? _____

    _____

2. "Whom you love." This is the first time the word "love" is used in the Bible. How are God the Father and Abraham similar in this respect (John 5:20)? _____

    How is their love different? _____

    _____

3. In what way was Isaac more than just a son? _____

    In what way was Jesus more than just a Son? _____

4. What would the loss of Isaac mean for Abraham? _____

5. How can anyone love God so much that they would be willing to sacrifice their own child? _____

   How can God love us so much that He would be willing to sacrifice His only Son? _____

6. How does God test our loyalty to Him in these passages?

   Matthew 10:37 _____

   Mark 8:38 _____

   1 Corinthians 10:13 _____

   Acts 14:22b _____

7. What two truths are stressed in Romans 8:31? _____

Genesis 22:3-14 The Obedience

1. God demanded Abraham's only son. And then Abraham, quietly and deliberately, made preparations to be obedient. He did not argue or question God's right to put him to this severe test. As a man of great faith and willing obedience, he immediately set out to do God's will. Remember that this entire story is filled with deep spiritual meaning.

   (a) Why was Abraham willing to sacrifice his only son? _____

   _____

   (b) How is our heavenly Father like Abraham according to Romans 8:32? _____

   (c) What does this tell you about *your value* to your heavenly Father? _____

2. Moriah was a mountain range at Jerusalem about 45 miles north of Beersheba. Mount Moriah was a hill in Jerusalem where Solomon would later build the Temple. Here the Israelites would offer sacrifices. Mount Moriah also seems to include the hill of Calvary where Jesus was crucified. Observe the profound symbolical significance of the entire

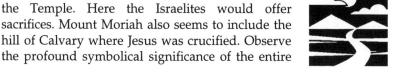

event. The wood for the sacrifice was placed on _____ The wooden cross for *the sacrifice* was placed on _____ As they approached Moriah Isaac asked where the lamb was, and Abraham replied that God would provide one. When they reached the top of Mount Moriah Isaac discovered that he was the offering. There seems to be no indication that he in any way resisted, but submitted willingly.

3. Abraham built the altar and placed wood on it. He bound Isaac and placed him on the altar. He took the knife, raised it high above his head, and was ready to plunge it into Isaac. At that very moment "the angel of the Lord" intervened and saved Isaac's life. Abraham had passed the supreme test. The angel is not a celestial being, but the preincarnate Christ. The Lord tells Abraham not to harm the boy. "Now I know that you fear God."

   (a) What might be some of the "Isaac(s)" that you need to surrender to God (give this considerable thought and discussion)? _____

   _____

   (b) How will you surrender them (try to be specific)? _____

   _____

   (c) Why must this be taken care of quickly? _____

   _____

4. The Lord, who Himself would become a Lamb to take away the sin of the world, provided a ram as a substitute for Isaac. Isaiah 53:4-5 reads: "Surely He (the Lamb of God) took up our infirmities and carried our sorrows, yet we considered Him stricken by God, smitten by Him, and afflicted. But He was pierced for our transgressions, He was crushed for our iniquities; the punishment that brought us peace was upon Him, and by His wounds we are healed." God has powerfully provided a Substitute for us!

Genesis 22:15-19 The Covenant Reconfirmed

The Lord appears to Abraham again and swears by Himself (the highest oath there is) that Abraham will be a source of blessing to the world. A great nation, Israel, will come into being from which the Messiah will come. The Lord promises victories over the enemies of God's chosen people. Verse 18 is definitely Messianic. "Offspring" is

"Seed" in the singular, one single Seed, namely, God's Son. St. Paul writes in Galatians 3:16: "The promises were spoken to Abraham and to his seed. The Scripture does not say 'and to seeds,' meaning many people, but 'and to your seed,' meaning one person, who is Christ." Abraham's faith is rewarded in a most wonderful manner. With his servants and Isaac he returns in joy to Beersheba.

1. In what respects was Jesus like Isaac? _____

_____

2. How do you suppose Abraham felt about this entire experience before, during, and after? _____

_____

3. How do you suppose Isaac felt about this experience before, during, and after? _____

_____

4. What did God discover about Abraham from this test? _____

_____

5. What did Abraham learn about God? _____

_____

6. What do you think Isaac learned about both of them? _____

_____

7. Why does God test His children at times? _____

_____

8. Think of a time of testing in your life. How did you feel about it at the time? _____

In what ways did you grow because of this test? _____

_____

What did you learn about yourself? _____

What did you learn about God? _____

_____

9. How does this Bible study help you better understand the decision

God faced in sacrificing His only Son for you? _____

---

10. Some of the more important gifts that you possess at this time may be the following: a family member (parent, spouse, child), money, a pet, TV set, computer, food, sports, friends, health, education, job, and God. On the line below arrange these items starting with those of least importance and ending with those of greater importance to you. The last item listed would be the number one item you would not want to part with under any circumstances:

_____

_____

_____

_____

11. What would you be willing to give up to remain faithful to God?

_____

_____

12. Now for some encouragement. Let's read it together: "No temptation has seized you except what is common to man. And God is faithful; He will not let you be tempted beyond what you can bear. But when you are tempted, He will also provide a way out so that you can stand up under it" (1 Corinthians 10:13).

Let's Wrap It Up

1. This lesson teaches me that God _____

_____

2. This lesson teaches me that Abraham _____

_____

3. This lesson teaches me that I (truths) _____

_____

(actions) _____

Closing Prayer

Closing Hymn

In the old rugged cross, stained with blood so divine,
A wondrous beauty I see; For 'twas on that old cross
Jesus suffered and died To pardon and Sanctify me.
Chorus:
So I'll cherish the old rugged cross,
'Till my trophies at last I lay down;
I will cling to the old rugged cross,
And exchange it some day for a crown.

To the old rugged cross I will ever be true,
Its shame and reproach gladly bear;
Then He'll call me some day to my home far away,
Where His glory forever I'll share. *Chorus:*

Bible Reading Schedule for the Next Seven Days

- ❑ 1st day – Genesis 29
- ❑ 2nd day – Genesis 30
- ❑ 3rd day – Genesis 31
- ❑ 4th day – Genesis 32
- ❑ 5th day – Genesis 33
- ❑ 6th day – Genesis 34
- ❑ 7th day – Genesis 35

Lesson 6

A TIME TO LAUGH... OR CRY

When Jacob Received
The Biggest Blessing

Genesis 25:21-34; 17:1-42; 28:1-4,10-19

Accounts of traffic accidents as the driver explained his particular accident to the officer:

"The accident occurred when I was attempting to bring my car out of a skid by steering it into the other vehicle."

"This guy was all over the place. I had to swerve a number of times before I hit him."

"A pedestrian hit me and went under my car."

"I was on my way to the doctor's with rear end trouble when my universal joint gave way causing me to have an accident."

"To avoid hitting the bumper of the car in front, I struck the pedestrian."

"My car was legally parked as it backed into the other vehicle."

"The pedestrian had no idea which direction to go, so I ran him over."

The officers undoubtedly didn't know whether to laugh or cry hearing these stories. That's about the way it is in this Bible study. Despite the deceit and lying, Jacob received the biggest blessing while Esau, Isaac, and Rebekah sinned also. Who can understand God's grace toward such sin, including ours? What a God we have!

Opening Hymn

We are climbing Jacob's ladder, We are climbing Jacob's ladder,
We are climbing Jacob's ladder, Soldiers of the cross.

Sinner, do you love my Jesus? Sinner, do you love my Jesus?
Sinner, do you love my Jesus? Soldiers of the cross.

Opening Prayer

Heavenly Father, as we study Esau, Jacob, and their family we see lying, deceit, and placing worldly things in front of spiritual things. We have done this in our lives, too. Please forgive us. We ask this solely because of Your love for us in Jesus who died on the cross to take away our sins. We want direction from You for our lives. We want to put heavenly things first. We want to have a "Bethel experience" with You in church each Sunday and as we study Your Word each day at home. May we daily sense Your presence. Send Your holy angels to protect us from all harm until that day that we shall be carried by them to be with Abraham, Isaac, Jacob, and all the saints in heaven. In Jesus' name. Amen.

Genesis 25:21-34 The Twins and the Birthright

1. God finally answered the prayer of Isaac for a child. Rebekah became pregnant with twins, but the babies struggled with each other even before birth. This served to indicate the clash between the spiritually renewed man of faith (Jacob) and the renewed natural man of the earth without faith (Esau). These two sons were, from their conception, two separate and different characters who would war with one another indefinitely. But there is much, much more.

    In Romans 9:5,11 Paul writes: "Theirs are the patriarchs (Isaac, Abraham, and Jacob – notice, not Esau, but Jacob), and from them is traced the human ancestry of Christ... Yet, before the twins were born or had done anything good or bad – in order that *God's purpose in election* might stand." Here God states that He elected or chose Jacob, not Esau, to receive the promise of the Messiah.

2. God knew both sons and chose (elected) Jacob. Esau proved to be stubborn and unregenerate. And so we read in Malachi 1:2-3: "I have loved Jacob, but Esau I have hated, and I have turned his mountains into a wasteland and left his inheritance to the desert jackals." Jacob is freely loved, and Esau is justly hated. "Esau" means "hairy." His name and physical appearance were "wild and wooly" as were his descendants, the Edomites. "Jacob" in Hebrew is related to the word "heel" which today is associated with deception which was one of his sins.

3. The two boys were opposites. Parental favoritism was obvious and added to the tension. Despite Jacob's lapses into sin he believed that God would continue the promise of the Messiah through his lineage. Jacob was committed to the Lord while Esau was not.

4. When Jacob was cooking stew Esau came in from the field hungry. "Sell me your birthright." The birthright was given the oldest son when the father died. This son would receive twice as much of the inheritance as each of the other children, would succeed the father as the head of the family, and, in this instance, would inherit God's promise given to Abraham of Canaan and of the ancestry of the Messiah.

    "What good is the birthright to me" indicates that Esau had no sense of values and no sensitivity for spiritual values. He was more concerned about his craving for food than he was in receiving earthly and everlasting blessings. Our sinful flesh also finds it appealing to compromise our eternal salvation for the passing material gain of this world.

    (a) Hebrews 12:16-17 reads: "See that no one is sexually immoral, or is godless like Esau, who for a single meal sold his inheritance rights as the oldest son. Afterward, as you know, when he wanted to inherit this blessing, he was rejected. He could bring about no change of mind, though he sought the blessing with tears." What two truths are stressed in these words? _____

    _____

    (b) What is our spiritual birthright? _____

45

(c) 1 John 2:15 says: "Do not love the world or anything in the world. If anyone loves the world, the love of the Father is not in him." When are we in danger of "selling" our spiritual birthright? _____

(d) In Mark 8:36-37 Jesus says: "What good is it for a man to gain the whole world, yet forfeit his soul? Or what can a man give in exchange for his soul?" What is the answer to Jesus' first question? _____ What is the answer to His second question? _____ _____ On the basis of these two answers why would we even consider the exchange? _____

(e) True or False: Despite Jacob's unworthy behavior, he still had faith in the promises of God.

(f) Was Esau entitled to the blessing his father wanted to give him?

(g) What mistake did Isaac and Rebecca make according to 25:28?

Deception

A tightwad visited a gift shop to find an inexpensive gift for a business associate, but he found everything too expensive until he spotted a vase which had been broken. He bought it for practically nothing and asked the store to send it, assuming his friend would think it had been broken in transit. In a few days he received an acknowledgment: "Many thanks for the vase," it read, "and it was so thoughtful of you to wrap each piece separately."

Genesis 27:1-42 The Great Deception

1. At this time Isaac was 137 years old. He thought the end was near, but he would live 40 years longer. He had one more important task to perform: to bestow the divine blessing given to Abraham, then

to himself, and now on to one of his sons. Blinded by his love for Esau, he forgot or ignored what God said in 25:23 – that Jacob was to receive this blessing. His favoritism for Esau encouraged Rebekah's silly scheme. She felt she had to take things into her own hands to "help God out." She plotted with Jacob in deceiving Isaac so that he would bless Jacob instead of Esau.

(a) Were Rebekah and Jacob right in deceiving Isaac? _____

(b) True or False: All four persons involved were equally guilty of wrong doing.

(c) What shall we say about "the end justifies the means? _____

_____

(d) What should Rebekah have done in this situation? _____

_____

(e) What should you do when you do not have a solution for a problem? _____

(f) Would you say Isaac and His family had a happy home life? Why? _____

_____

2. After three outright lies by Jacob, Isaac unknowingly gave the Messianic blessing to him. When Esau appeared later, Isaac began to tremble at what had happened. The blessing had now been given and could not be changed or retracted. This is the second time Esau was deprived of the birthright, but he did not repent of his unbelief.

"Esau... burst out with a loud and bitter cry." Here is the fruit of unbelief. Tragically he pleaded, "Haven't you any blessing for me?" Again we read, "Esau wept aloud." Esau and his descendants would get something – a hard lot! They would live far away from the fruit field fields of Canaan in sterile deserts. They became Edomites. Herod the Great was a descendant of Esau. The Arabians who are Muhammadans and bitter enemies of the Jews are at least in part descended from Esau.

(a) True or False: Belief and unbelief have their rewards already in this life. Reaping always follows sowing in due time.

(b) Isaac asked God to give Jacob three blessings. What were they?

Genesis 28:1-4 Isaac Blesses Jacob

Esau's heart is filled with anger toward Jacob, and he resolves to murder him after the death of his father. Rebekah urges Jacob to flee to her brother Laban in Mesopotamia where he could find a God-fearing wife. Isaac approves of Rebekah's plans, and welcomes Jacob with kindness and thoughtfulness. Before sending him on his journey Isaac repeats the Messianic blessing to Jacob. Isaac, without question, now recognizes Jacob as the chosen heir.

Genesis 28:10-19 Jacob's Dream at Bethel

The distance from Beersheba to Bethel is about 55 miles and to Haran over 500 miles. One evening, during his sleep, Jacob has a vision of a ladder reaching from earth to heaven. God wants Jacob to know that His plan for him would not fail. Angels ascend and descend the ladder symbolizing the constant presence and protection of guardian angels. This is the first appearance of the Lord to Jacob – there were seven all together. The Lord repeats the promises given to Abraham and Isaac concerning their physical descendants and out of them that one Seed, the promised Savior.

Jacob awakes from the dream filled with awe. He knew that the Lord was there. Jacob calls the place Bethel (House of God) and vows that he will return to build a permanent memorial to God's grace. He vows (this is the first instance of a vow in the Bible) to be faithful to the Lord and to give Him one tenth of all the material blessings that come to him. Time to laugh!

1. What makes our church a "house of God" and the "gate of heaven"? _____

   What effect should the above have on our attendance and behavior in church? _____

   Many people who do not attend church today say they can be Christians without church attendance. Are they correct? Why?

Try to name just one believer in the Bible who did not worship and study with other believers: _____

2. The "Bethel experience" reassured Jacob that God and the holy angels would be with him. What helps you feel that way today?

_____

3. When will we see heaven open and angels ascending and descending (John 1:51)? _____

4. Hebrews 1:1-2 says: "In the past God spoke to our forefathers through the prophets at many times and in various ways, but in these last days He has spoken to us by His Son." Do you agree with some people who claim that God still speaks through visions and dreams? _____ Why? _____

_____

5. This is the second Bible reference on voluntary tithing. Why did Jacob and why do some Christians today voluntarily tithe?

_____

6. God is a God of love and mercy. He often forgives and blesses people who are far from perfect. Think of your own life. When are you glad that God forgives you? _____

_____

7. God promised to be with Jacob and his descendants. Write the words of a similar promise Jesus gives you in Matthew 28:20:

_____

Let's Wrap It Up

1. This lesson teaches me that God _____

_____

2. This lesson teaches me that Jacob _____

_____

3. This lesson teaches me that I (truths) _____

_____

(actions) _____

Closing Prayer

Closing Hymn

If you love Him, why not serve Him? If you love Him, why not serve Him? If you love Him, why not serve Him? Soldiers of the cross.

Rise and shine and give God glory, Rise and shine and give God glory, Rise and shine and give God glory, Soldiers of the cross.

Bible Reading Schedule for the Next Seven Days

❑ 1st day – Genesis 36   ❑ 5th day – Genesis 40
❑ 2nd day – Genesis 37   ❑ 6th day – Genesis 41
❑ 3rd day – Genesis 38   ❑ 7th day – Genesis 42
❑ 4th day – Genesis 39

Lesson 7

A TIME TO LAUGH... OR CRY

With Joseph the Slave,
the Prisoner, the Prime Minister

Genesis 37:3-11,26-28,36; 39:1-23; 40:1-23; 41:1-56; 46:1-7

Just who and what are saints? I asked a six year boy who he thought the saints were. He replied, "Oh, they are the football players at New Orleans." Another person responded, "Saints are dead people." Six year old Mark made a visit to a large Cathedral in Washington, D.C. where he saw many beautiful stained glass windows. The lives of the saints were portrayed in magnificent colors. Since his family had not discussed this subject before, his father asked him what a saint was. He responded, "It's a person with the light shining through him." Now we're getting close. In this lesson we're going to study one of the greatest saints in the Old Testament – Joseph. Although the Messianic promises were not given to him, his life was typical of our Savior's life. Like Jesus, Joseph first passed through a period of humiliation and suffering and then rose to a state of honor and glory.

Opening Hymn

For all the saints who from their labors rest,
All who by faith before the world confessed,
Your name, O Jesus, be forever blest. Alleluia! Alleluia!

You were their rock, their fortress, and their might;
You, Lord, their Captain in the well-fought fight;
You, in the darkness drear, their one true light. Alleluia! Alleluia!

Opening Prayer

Dear Lord, we thank You for the story of Joseph the slave, the prisoner, and the prime minister which we are about to study. You permitted him to go through very difficult times, yet, You remained his strength and His God. Forgive us for the times we have complained about the way people treat us and about circumstances which take place in our lives which we think are unfair. Help us know and believe that You are always with us, that You love us and protect us, and that You are presenting to us ways in which we can demonstrate our trust in You. Assist us to become more helpful toward those who are hurting. We believe that with You as our Savior we can do all things. We pray in Your name. Amen.

Genesis 37:3-11,26-28 Joseph Sold

1. Joseph is presented as honest, handsome, capable, and very faithful to God, perhaps the most-loved character in the Old Testament. At this time he is about seventeen years old, and he is Jacob's favorite son. He tattles on the wickedness of his brothers; they, of course, hate him. The robe is a beautiful, colorful cloak normally worn by an exceptional class of people as a mark of distinction; frequently it included gold and other ornamental applique. How do parents today make mistakes similar to that which Jacob made? _____

2. God frequently revealed knowledge in the Old Testament through dreams. Today He reveals His will to us through the written Word. Should we attach any significance to our dreams today? _____

Joseph's dreams were prophetic and divinely inspired. The first dream indicated that he would rule over his brothers and the second dream that he would rule over all the house of Israel. Jacob sensed that there was something special about the dreams; to keep them from going to Joseph's head Jacob gave him a polite reprimand. Twenty-two years later everyone involved saw the dreams come true. But the brothers now hated Joseph intensely.

3. The hatred turns to plans for murder, but Reuben, perhaps feeling accountable to his father, talks the brothers out of it. They throw Joseph into an empty cistern. Finally they hit on the idea of selling him to passing Midianite merchants. The price is twenty pieces of silver which was less than the price of a common slave. Surely this was not a time for Joseph to laugh, but he remained faithful to God. Watch how, at the right moment, God turns the evil into good.

Genesis 39:1-23 The Temptation

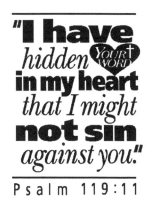

"I have *hidden* **in my heart** *that I might* **not sin** *against you."*

Psalm 119:11

Joseph was sold to Potiphar, Pharaoh's chief bodyguard. Here Joseph would learn the Egyptian language and customs and develop the administrative ability which he would need later on. The Lord was with him, and everything he did met with success.

Potiphar's wife repeatedly tried to seduce Joseph. He had three reasons why he would not commit fornication: 1. It would be a betrayal toward his master who trusted him. 2. Potiphar's wife belong to Potiphar. 3. His sin would also be against God whom he loved. In anger she took his cloak as "evidence."

Potiphar may have suspected his wife. Death was the normal penalty in a case like this. Instead, Joseph was put in prison. The Lord stayed with him there. So blessed was this man by the Lord that the warden put everything in prison under Joseph's care. Affliction is often God's way to great blessing.

1. Why was Joseph so respected and trusted in Egypt? _____

_____

2. When is a Christian a real success in life? _____

3. What have you learned so far about Joseph's character? _____

Genesis 40:1-23 More Dreams

God's providence continued to work to fulfill a divine plan through Joseph. The cupbearer and baker were not lowly servants, but court officials. Each of them had dreams placed in their minds by Joseph's God. When Joseph saw their sad faces he inquired as to the cause of their gloom. They responded that they had dreams and didn't understand them. Joseph suggested that God can interpret them. "Tell me your dreams."

"Pharaoh will lift up your head" is an expression with a reverse meaning. The cupbearer will be pardoned and restored in three days, and the baker will lose his head and his body will be hung from a tree (birds eating out of a basket on his head indicates the same thing). While Joseph asked the cupbearer to remember him upon his release, he forgot about Joseph.

1. Was it to Joseph's advantage that he had to spend years in prison? Why? _____

2. What can we learn from Joseph concerning the use of our abilities?

    _____

3. Show how we may be able to serve God and our fellow men even under difficult circumstances: _____

    _____

4. Suppose Joseph would have given up hope and refused to be a faithful servant in Potiphar's house and later in prison. What kind of a person do you think he would have turned out to be? _____

    _____

Genesis 41:1-56 The Prime Minister

Two years later Joseph is still in jail. He is unwavering in his loyalty to God. Egypt is one of the most fruitful countries in the world. The fertile soil produced huge crops of wheat when irrigated with the water from the Nile. Egyptians worship the Nile as a god. The cow is also sacred to them. Pharaoh's first dream concerns cows and a second dream deals with wheat, but all the magicians and wise men in Egypt cannot interpret them.

The cupbearer shares his story of dream interpretation by Joseph. Joseph is summoned. He declares that God alone can reveal the future. Then he proceeds with the interpretation. Both dreams have the same meaning. There will be seven years of plenty followed by seven years of famine.

Joseph advises Pharaoh on steps that should be taken to avoid catastrophe during the famine. The king should appoint a man with ability and wisdom to erect huge granaries and gather a fifth of the crops during the years of plenty.

Immediately the king appoints Joseph the prime minister of all Egypt; only the king will be over him. He is given a white robe, a gold chain, a royal chariot, and full authority. He is given a wife and is blessed with two sons, Manasseh ("forgetting") and Ephraim ("double fruitfulness"). The grain is saved, and many lives are spared. Question: Since there is a good and all-powerful God in heaven, why does He permit evil to happen? Answer: _____

Genesis 46:1-7 Jacob Moves to Egypt

The famine spreads all the way to Canaan where Jacob's family learns that food can be purchased in Egypt. The brothers make the trip. Joseph recognizes them and treats them kindly with instructions to go back to Canaan to get their father Jacob.

God assures Jacob that it is His will that he make the trip. God will protect him on the way, renew the promise of a great nation, accomplish the return of Israel to Canaan, and reunite him with Joseph. Joseph places them in Goshen, a fertile land in the delta of the Nile. There they develop into a separate nation from which the Messiah finally comes. It is time for them to laugh.

1. What is the most admirable thing about Joseph? _____

   _____

2. What do you think Joseph's profession would be if he lived today?

   _____

3. What happens to Joseph's faith during all of his experiences in Egypt? _____

4   Why do you think Joseph decided to be a faithful servant instead of giving up (Remember that he didn't know Pharaoh would make him the No. 2 man in the country)? _____

_____

5. How could Joseph forgive his brothers and Potiphar's wife the things they did to him? _____
How can you learn to be more forgiving toward those who hurt you? _____

_____

6. What situations in life make you feel fearful? _____

_____ What can you learn from Joseph to help you? _____

7. Genesis 15:13-14: "Then the LORD said to him, 'Know for certain that your descendants will be strangers in a country not their own, and they will be enslaved and mistreated four hundred years. But I will punish the nation they serve as slaves, and afterward they will come out with great possessions.'" What important prophecy do you find here?

_____

_____

_____

Just as you have received Christ Jesus as Lord, continue to live in Him.
Colossians 2:6

8. In what ways was Joseph like Jesus? _____

_____

_____

_____

_____

9. Comment on this statement: "If you are faithful, God will help you, and you will always succeed." _____

_____

10. How can we, like Joseph, be a blessing to others? _____

_____

11. Through all of Joseph's life God was in control even though it did not seem so at times. The events which occurred, including the suffering, took place for the good of many people. Jesus had to suffer, too. He was brought to the prison house of hell to accomplish our salvation. God had a plan for Joseph, a plan for Jesus, and He has a plan for me. When I understand that plan or at least move with it by faith, I can learn to laugh with Joseph. Which of the two points in the last sentence are most important? Why?

_____

Let's Wrap It Up

1. This lesson teaches me that God _____

_____

2. This lesson teaches me that Joseph _____

_____

3. This lesson teaches me that I (truths) _____

_____

(actions) _____

_____

Closing Prayer

Closing Hymn

Oh, may Your soldiers, faithful, true, and bold,
Fight as the saints who nobly fought of old;
And win with them the victor's crown of gold. Alleluia! Alleluia!

But then there breaks a yet more glorious day:
The saints triumphant rise in bright array;
The King of glory passes on His way. Alleluia! Alleluia!

From earth's wide bounds, from ocean's farthest coast,
Through gates of pearl stream in the countless host,
Singing to Father, Son, and Holy Ghost. Alleluia! Alleluia!

Bible Reading Schedule for the Next Seven Days

- ❑ 1st day – Genesis 43
- ❑ 2nd day – Genesis 44
- ❑ 3rd day – Genesis 45
- ❑ 4th day – Genesis 46
- ❑ 5th day – Genesis 47
- ❑ 6th day – Genesis 48
- ❑ 7th day – Genesis 49,50

Lesson 8

A TIME TO LAUGH... OR CRY

When God Called Moses
to Lead Israel

Exodus 1:5-10,22; 2:1-10,23-25; 3:1-15; 4:1-17,19-31

The church secretary answered the phone. The gentleman on the other end said: "May I speak to the head of the hog trough?" The secretary said, "Who?" He repeated: "The head of the hog trough." She said, "Sir, we treat our minister with respect. We call him 'Pastor' or 'Reverend.'" Then he said, "Well, I was thinking of giving $25,000 to the building fund." There was silence, and then she said, "Sir, the pig just walked in!" What an accommodating secretary. Her pastor "head of the hog trough"? Normally she would never consent to the thought, but for $25,000, well, why not? In some ways she reminds us of another of God's workers, Moses – who, at times, was even more accommodating. He wanted to act in his own strength, and later he didn't want to act at all, and there was a lot more involved than $25,000. Then God had His way. Abraham and God laughed and cried; it's important that we know why.

Opening Hymn

My faith looks up to Thee, Thou Lamb of Calvary,
Savior divine! Now hear me while I pray, Take all my guilt away,
O let me from this day Be wholly Thine!

May Thy rich grace impart Strength to my fainting heart,
My zeal inspire; As Thou hast died for me, O may my love to Thee
Pure, warm, and changeless be, A living fire!

Opening Prayer

Almighty God, You graciously heard the cry of Your people in their bondage in Egypt. You called Moses to be their leader even though he was self-accommodating. You revealed Your name and Yourself to Moses and Your people. Give us faith to see Your love and help in our lives. Especially when we are in difficulty, strengthen our confidence in You. Thank You for sending Jesus to be our Savior and that He leads us from sin and death to the Promised Land of Heaven. Help us be Your "Moses" to many people today who are in slavery to sin and the devil. May we tell them about Your name and Jesus and how they can become Your people. May this study and the days ahead of us be a time of happiness and laughter with You. In Jesus' name. Amen.

Exodus 1:5-10,22 Growth of Israel

From seventy people who entered Egypt with Jacob around 1876 B.C., a large nation of about two million people came into being 430 years later. God used Egypt to form Jacob's family into this mighty nation from which the Savior would come. The Israelites grew in number in the land of Goshen. A new king put them into forced labor. Then the order was given that every baby boy was to be killed. What

similar situation happened in Jesus' day? _____

_____

Pharaoh's plot to exterminate the Israelites served to implement God's plan to liberate His people. This is a record of the Lord of history in action, moving toward His announced goal to free His people and bring them to the Promised Land.

Exodus 2:1-10 Birth of Moses

 Moses' parents were Amram and Jochebed (6:20) of the tribe of Levi which was later selected as the priestly line. Hebrews 11:23 reads: "By faith Moses' parents hid him for three months after he was born, because they saw he was no ordinary child, and they were not afraid of the king's edict." What is it that prompted Moses' parents to develop a plan to save him? _____

The basket was made of papyrus reed woven together and sealed with bitumen (pitch), a well-known product from the Dead Sea. By divine guidance Pharaoh's daughter rescued the baby from the river. She called him Moses *(Mosheh)*, meaning "the one drawing out." Moses was drawn out of the water to draw God's people out of slavery and lead them to the Promised Land. Jesus Christ was drawn out of heaven to draw us out of slavery to sin and everlasting hell and lead us to the real Promised Land of Heaven.

Exodus 2:23-25 Covenant Remembered

The oppression of the Israelites continued under a new king. Their cries went up to God. He did not forget His promise. He looked on the Israelites with compassion. The time for divine intervention was getting close. What was God's purpose for permitting His people to suffer in Egypt? _____

_____

Why does God allow His people today to suffer affliction and oppression?_____

_____

Exodus 3:1-15 The Call of Moses

1. When Moses was forty years old he felt that it was time to strike the first blow (2:11-12) to deliver the Israelites. He acted, however, before God told him to. He therefore had to spend forty years in

exile herding sheep (a vocation the Egyptians despised) in the country of Midian. If possible, scan Acts 7:20-38. This proved to be a long but rewarding training period for the future leader. Discuss: Why is it wise to insist that future pastors (shepherds) go through a rather lengthy period of training (6 to 8 years) before they begin

serving? _____

_____

Hebrews 11:24-26 reads: "By faith Moses, when he had grown up, refused to be known as the son of Pharaoh's daughter. He chose to be mistreated along with the people of God rather than to enjoy the pleasures of sin for a short time. He regarded disgrace for the sake of Christ as of greater value than the treasures of Egypt, because he was looking ahead to his reward." What big things do these words

tell us about Moses? _____

_____

_____

2. Moses was tending sheep in the desert when the call came. The "angel of the Lord" was the preincarnate Son of God. He appeared in the form of fire in a burning bush. Fire was often used to symbolize divine presence and is a reminder of His holiness. Moses was to realize the chasm between himself and a holy God by taking off his sandals. The ground was holy ground. He hid his face, afraid to look at God. God was going to carry out His promise made first to Adam and Eve (Genesis 3:15) and repeated to Abraham, Isaac, and Jacob. He had chosen Moses to lead Israel out of bondage to the Promised Land.

3. Moses asks what God's name is. "I am who I am." "I AM." The name comes from the Hebrew *haya* "to be." God has no name like Apollo or Zeus. No human mind can explain Him. He cannot be defined. He is different from anyone or anything. I AM means that God is the Creator of life. He rules all. He never changes. He keeps His promises.

Moses is to go in the name of "The Lord." God would be known by a name which differentiated Him from all other gods: LORD. From the four Hebrew consonants WHWH with the vowels of the word for Lord the name "Jehovah" or "Yahweh" came into use. God's name is recorded frequently in the Old Testament and signifies the entirety of His revelation to His chosen family. What God was in the Old Testament is fulfilled when Jesus revealed God's name to mankind during His three year ministry. How do you account for the lack of reverence for God's name by many Christians today?

_____

What can we do to increase respect for God's name in our lives?

_____

Exodus 4:1-17,29-31 Signs for Moses

1. Years before, Moses was eager to lead Israel in his own strength. Now he is unwilling to do it *with* God's strength. Moses was afraid that Israel would not follow him as their deliverer. The Lord gave him three signs to substantiate his claim. First the Lord changed Moses' staff to a snake. The second sign was a healthy hand turned leprous and then turned healthy again. The third sign would turn water into blood. Moses was a self-accommodating man. What excuses did Moses give God? How did God respond?

   First excuse (3:11-12): _____

   God replied: _____

   Second excuse (3:13-15): _____

   God replied: _____

   Third excuse (4:1-9): _____

   God replied: _____

   Fourth excuse (4:10-17): _____

   God replied: _____

   What are some common excuses God's people give today for not

   working for Him?_____

   What are some of God's replies? _____

   _____

2. The Lord is angry with Moses. Do you suppose God is ever angry

   about some of our excuses? Why? _____

   _____

In mercy God provided Moses with a helper, his brother Aaron. They had been separated for 40 years. Moses was 80 now, and Aaron was 83. God would speak to Moses. Moses would speak to

Aaron. And Aaron would speak to the people.

3. "Dear Church Member: This is a chain letter meant to bring happiness to you. Unlike other chain letters, it does not cost money. Simply send a copy of this letter to six other churches who are tired of their pastors. Then bundle up your pastor and send him to the church at the bottom of the list. In a week you will receive 16,436 pastors, and one of them should be a dandy. Have faith in this letter. One man broke the chain and got his old pastor back!" This brings a smile to most pastors and people.

(a) Israel had a lot of ups and downs with Moses just like you do with your pastor. Why is that

(for Israel and for you)? _____

_____

_____

(b) How would Israel have faired with-

out a Moses? _____

_____

(c) How well would you do spiritually without the holy ministry? _____ Why? _____

_____

(d) In what ways is your pastor a "Moses" to you? _____

_____

4. Why did the Lord allow Moses to perform signs for Israel? _____

_____ Acts 8:6 reads: "When the crowds heard Philip and saw the miraculous signs he did, they all paid close attention to what he said." Why did the Lord allow the apostles to

perform signs? _____

Matthew 12:38-42 is significant: "Then some of the Pharisees and teachers of the law said to Him, 'Teacher, we want to see a miraculous sign from You.' He answered, 'A wicked and adulterous generation asks for a miraculous sign! But none will be given it except the sign of the prophet Jonah. For as Jonah was three days and three nights in the belly of a huge fish, so the Son of Man will be three days and three nights in the heart of the earth. The men of Nineveh will stand up at the judgment with this generation and condemn it; for they repented at the preaching of Jonah, and now One greater than Jonah is here. The Queen of the South will rise at the judgment with this generation and condemn it; for she came from the ends of the earth to listen to Solomon's wisdom, and now One greater than Solomon is here.'" What is Jesus really saying

here? _____

_____

_____

5. As Moses stood between God and Israel, Jesus stands between God and you.

    (a) 1 Timothy 2:5-6: "For there is one God and one mediator between God and men, the man Christ Jesus, who gave Himself as a ransom for all men." What does Jesus do for you here?

    _____

    (b) 1 John 2:1-2: "My dear children, I write this to you so that you will not sin. But if anybody does sin, we have One who speaks to the Father in our defense -- Jesus Christ, the Righteous One. He is the atoning sacrifice for our sins, and not only for ours but also for the sins of the whole world." What does Jesus do

    here? _____

    (c) What should (a) and (b) mean to you? _____

    _____

6. The people believed when they saw the signs. God was ready to act in their best interests, and they believed it. They bowed down and worshiped. What a God! Time to laugh! That God is our God today.

    Why does God love mankind so much? _____

Let's Wrap It Up

1. This story teaches me that God _____

_____

2. This story teaches me that Moses _____

_____

3. This story teaches me that Israel _____

4. This story teaches me that I (truths) _____

_____

(actions) _____

_____

Closing Prayer

Closing Hymn

While life's dark maze I tread And griefs around me spread,
Be Thou my guide; Bid darkness turn to day,
Wipe sorrow's tears away, Nor let me ever stray From Thee aside.

When ends life's passing dream, When death's cold, threatening stream
Shall o'er me roll, Blest Savior, then, in love,
Fear and distrust remove; O lift me safe above, A ransomed soul!

Bible Reading Schedule for the Next Seven Days

- ❏ 1st day – Exodus 1
- ❏ 2nd day – Exodus 2
- ❏ 3rd day – Exodus 3
- ❏ 4th day – Exodus 4
- ❏ 5th day – Exodus 5
- ❏ 6th day – Exodus 6
- ❏ 7th day – Exodus 7

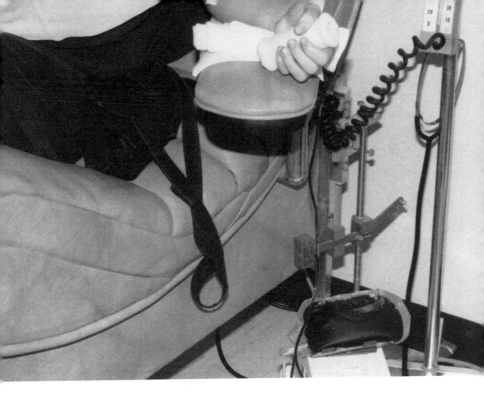

A TIME TO LAUGH... OR CRY

When Israel Was Saved
by the Blood of a Lamb

Exodus 11:1-10; 12:1-50

One of the most important substances in the human body is the blood. We cannot live without it. Each of us has about five quarts circulating every twenty-three seconds so that every cell in our body is supplied with food and cleansed at the same time. The Bible calls blood the life of the flesh. We are all related by blood to Adam. Blood is mentioned 460 times in the Bible. On the night of the Passover in Egypt God told the Hebrew people to put the blood of a slain lamb on the doorposts of each house. Death was coming that night to the firstborn in all the land of mankind and animals. "When I see the blood on the doorposts," said God, "I will pass over you." Not when God sees our good resolutions, not when He sees our tears, not when

He sees our agonies or our good works, but when He sees the blood of Jesus is there forgiveness and life, now and forever!

Opening Hymn

Jesus, Your blood and righteousness My beauty are, my glorious dress; Mid flaming worlds, in these arrayed, With joy shall I lift up my head.

Bold shall I stand in that great day, Cleansed and redeemed, no debt to pay; For by Your cross absolved I am From sin and guilt, from fear and shame.

Opening Prayer

Dear God, You could not tolerate the sin of the people who lived in Egypt. You cannot tolerate our sin today. You saved Israel in Egypt by having them take blood from a lamb and placing it on their doorposts. Help us see how this pointed forward to Jesus who shed His blood on a wooden cross to save a corrupt world from all of its sin. O Father, have mercy on us for the sake of Jesus. Help us do everything we can to explain to unbelievers that You will forgive their sins through Jesus' blood. We thank You for Your love and for Jesus. Bless us now in this Bible study. Amen.

Exodus 11:1-10 Death of Firstborn

1. Moses and Aaron had appeared before Pharaoh with the demand that he allow the Israelites to leave the country. Nine times this demand was repeated, and nine times God tried to break Pharaoh's stubborn resistance by means of a plague. The plagues only served to harden Pharaoh's heart against God.

    (a) True or False: When verse 8 says that Moses left Pharaoh "hot with anger," it was a holy and just anger because Pharaoh, despite all the communication and plagues, had rejected the Word of the Lord.

    (b) Pharaoh's "day of grace" had run out. What does that mean?

    _____

    (c) What is the difference between God's foreknowledge of evil (think of Pharaoh) and what God wills? _____

    _____

2. Ten devastating plagues were to come upon Egypt. They are described in Exodus 7-12. Tell what each plague was like in a few words.

(7:19) _____

(8:2) _____

(8:16) _____

(8:21) _____

(9:6) _____

(9:9) _____

(9:18) _____

(10:4) _____

(10:21) _____

(12:29) _____

3. The Lord told Moses he would bring one more plague (*nega*, a "blow" or "stroke"). Then Pharaoh would not just permit, but would drive the Israelites out. He also announced that the people would take the Egyptians' silver and gold, costly vessels, and jewelry, as a compensation for all their years of unpaid labor. Moses then announced the last catastrophic plague: the firstborn of man and beast throughout the land would die. Read verse 7 again. "Not a dog will bark" is another way of saying there will be no resistance to the exodus. First Pharaoh hardened his heart, and then God judicially hardened it.

(a) How do the Lord's judgments on Pharaoh serve as a lesson for

us today? _____

_____

(b) Why do we need to be careful about trying to understand why

certain catastrophes happen today? _____

_____

Exodus 12:1-13 The Passover

The plan of redemption and the birth of a nation required a change in the calendar. There was to be a new beginning.

The Passover commemorates the rescue of God's people out of Egypt. This memorial meal was to be kept perpetually by Israel. The lamb was slain at home, and the blood was painted on the doorposts. A lamb without blemish points forward to the sinless Savior. The angel of death would "pass over" only those people whose sins had been removed by substitutionary sacrifice. To show their need for forgiveness, the Israelites were to confess their sins. They were to show faith in God's promise of forgiveness of their sins by putting the blood of a lamb or goat on the two doorposts and lintel of their homes. Israel was to be ready to travel. Deliverance was near.

The slain lamb was a type of the Lamb of God who shed His holy blood on Calvary. Applying the blood symbolizes our applying Christ's blood to ourselves by faith. As the Israelites were shielded from death, so we are shielded from God's wrath. No bones were to be broken. See how this prophecy is fulfilled in John 19:33,36 – "When the soldiers came to Jesus and found that He was already dead, they did not break His legs... These things happened so that the Scripture would be fulfilled: 'Not one of His bones will be broken.'"

1. How did the Passover come to completion in the New Testament according to Hebrews 10:12-14? _____

2. What is the Passover changed to in Matthew 26:17-29? _____

3. Of what should we be reminded every time we see and celebrate the Lord's Supper? _____

Exodus 12:14-18 Feast of Unleavened Bread

The Passover commemorated the deliverance of believers on that dreadful night of death. The Feast of Unleavened Bread was to remind the people of their exodus from Egypt. Leaven is an illustration of sin. The Feast of Unleavened Bread lasted for seven days during which there could be no work except for the preparation of food. The Feast was to symbolize the consecration of the Israelites based on their redemption.

Exodus 12:29-32 The Tenth Plague

The lives of the firstborn of men and animals were snuffed out.

Pharaoh considered himself divine, but he could not prevent the death of his own son and that of the others. The firstborn were struck down in every case, in every family from the highest to the lowest. God's punishment spared none except where there was blood. A cry of distress arose throughout the land. Moses and Aaron were called before Pharaoh and urged to leave the country with their people.

1. Who do you suppose cried in Egypt that night and why? _____

_____

2. Who do you suppose rejoiced that night and why? _____

_____

3. Some people say they cannot harmonize the love of God with the death of Egypt's firstborn. What do they forget? _____

Exodus 12:33-42 The Exodus

Moses gives the number of people leaving at 600,000 men (Males 20 years old and older) together with the women and children. This would bring the total number to at least two million. Various foreigners also accompanied Israel. They had been in bondage for 430 years. The approximate date of the exodus is 1446 B.C. "From Rameses" where they lived in Egypt to "Succoth," the edge of the wilderness at that time toward the east to where the Suez Canal presently passes through.

Exodus 12:43-50 Passover Restrictions

1. Only the Lord's Covenant people were to partake of the Passover; all of them were to participate. Concerning Holy Communion 1 Corinthians 11:28-29 says: "A man ought to examine himself before he eats of the bread and drinks of the cup. For anyone who eats and drinks without recognizing the body of the Lord eats and drinks judgment on himself." Who should not participate in the

Sacrament of Holy Communion? _____

2. True or False: Except for the reasons given above, every Christian should always attend the Lord's Table when it is being served.

3. The Passover was to be a family observance. In what sense is this

still true today with the Lord Supper? _____

4. What do these verses tell us about blood?

Leviticus 17:11 _____

Hebrews 9:22 _____

1 John 1:7b _____

5. What might we say to people who are offended at the thought of salvation through Jesus' blood or as they call it: "blood theology"?

_____

6. Describe (according to 1 Peter 1:18-19) the Lamb who saves us:

_____

Let's Wrap It Up

1. This story teaches me that God _____

_____

2. This story teaches me that Israel _____

_____

3. This story teaches me that I (truths) _____

_____

(actions) _____

_____

Closing Prayer

Closing Hymn

Lord, I believe Your precious blood, Which at the mercy-seat of God Pleads for the captives' liberty, Was also shed in love for me.

When from the dust of death I rise To claim my mansion in the skies, This then shall be my only plea; Christ Jesus lived and died for me.

Bible Reading Schedule for the Next Seven Days

❑ 1st day – Exodus 8
❑ 2nd day – Exodus 9
❑ 3rd day – Exodus 10
❑ 4th day – Exodus 11

❑ 5th day – Exodus 12
❑ 6th day – Exodus 13
❑ 7th day – Exodus 14

Lesson 10

A TIME TO LAUGH... OR CRY

When God Gave the Law on Sinai

Exodus 19:1 - 20:21

The Ten Rules

1. The female always makes the rules. The rules are subject to change at any time without prior notification.
2. No male can possibly know all the rules.
3. If the female suspects the male knows all the rules, she must immediately change some or all of the rules.
4. The female is never wrong. If the female is wrong, it is because of a flagrant misunderstanding which was a direct result of something the male did or said wrong.
5. If Rule 4b applies, the male must apologize immediately for causing the misunderstanding.

6. The female can change her mind at any given point in time. The male must never change his mind without express written consent from the female.
7. The female has every right to be angry or upset at any time.
8. The male must remain calm at all times, unless the female wants him to be angry or upset.
9. The female must under no circumstances let the male know whether or not she wants him to be angry or upset.
10. Any attempt to alter these rules could result in severe bodily harm.

The Ten Commandments are not like the above Ten Rules over which we can laugh or at least the males can laugh. The Commandments are from a holy God. They tell us what to do and not do and how we are to be and not be. This lesson takes us to Sinai. Here God gave the Commandments to Moses and the people. It would be a time to laugh *and* cry!

Opening Hymn

Come, O almighty King, Help us Your name to sing; Help us to praise;
Father all glorious, In all victorious, Come and reign over us,
Ancient of Days.

Come, O incarnate Word, Gird on Your mighty sword; Our prayer attend. Come and Your people bless, And give Your Word success, And let Your righteousness On us descend.

Opening Prayer

Almighty God, Author of the holy Ten Commandments, we thank You for being a covenant God with Israel and with us. Like Israel, we have sinned against You in thought, word, and deed. Forgive us through Jesus' blood. Give us grace to put You first. Help us use the Commandments as a guide in our lives; we know this will result in a happier life as we serve You and others. Help us understand what happened when You gave the Commandments to Moses on two tablets of stone. Bless our study and our fellowship with each other and with You. In Jesus' name. Amen.

Exodus 19:1-9 Arrival at Sinai and First Message

1. The Israelites reached Sinai after three months of travel and remained there for about a year. Most scholars feel that Mount Sinai is the rugged peak now known as Jebel Musa, about 6,830 feet high.

Moses ascended the mountain to receive instructions from God. Israel was to be reminded that both their physical and spiritual salvation was an act of pure grace on the part of God. St. Paul informs us: "It is by grace you have been saved, through faith -- and this not from yourselves, it is the gift of God -- not by works, so that no one can boast" (Ephesians 2:8-9).

"I carried you on eagles' wings and brought you to Myself." A parent eagle, when teaching its young to fly, sometimes glides underneath them and bears them safely back to the nest again. This is a beautiful picture of God's utter and total love for Israel and for us. It's time for us to laugh and be happy in the Lord!

2. Words of love: "You will be My treasured possession!"

    (a) God speaks these words to me, too! I am His. He is mine. Why

    is this truth so slow in sinking in? _____

    (b) God's plan for Israel was a theocracy. God Himself would rule them. This was the only way they could be a "kingdom of

    priests." What do these three words mean? _____

    _____

    Write the words which show the people's response: _____

    _____

    (c) Underline the beautiful and special names God gives you: "But you are a chosen people, a royal priesthood, a holy nation, a people belonging to God, that you may declare the praises of Him who called you out of darkness into His wonderful light" (1 Peter 2:9).

    (d) How was God going to convince the people to trust and follow

    the leadership of Moses? _____

    (e) Why should we follow the leadership of our shepherd (pastor)?

    _____

Exodus 19:10-15 Special Instructions

The people were to consecrate themselves in preparation for the Lord's visit on the third day. The outward preparation was to signify their inner preparation. They were not to go near the mountain or to touch it; whoever disobeyed would die. A barrier was erected around the base of the mountain demonstrating the huge chasm which separates the Creator from His creatures. What outward preparation was to follow? _____

Exodus 19:16-25

"Thunder and lightning," "thick cloud," and "a very loud trumpet blast" were expressions by which God revealed Himself as holy. It was an audio visual lesson on His holiness in contrast to the sinfulness of men. What effect did it have on the people? _____

Exodus 20:1-17 The Ten Commandments

1. The many laws which were given to Israel can be divided into three groups. The MORAL LAW dealt with their relationship with God and people. The CEREMONIAL LAW decreed how Israel would worship God. The CIVIL LAW governed Israel as a nation under the direct rule of the Lord. The moral law was written in man's heart at creation and is binding on all people for all time.

   "God spoke." What He said is reported in the remaining chapters of Exodus, Leviticus, and Deuteronomy. These words can be summarized as follows: Israel was to realize that it was totally dependent on God's strength and mercy. Just as they were in physical slavery in Egypt, so they were in spiritual bondage. They did not deserve God's favor. They were to respond to God's love by obedience flowing out of faith. By this obedience Israel would give evidence of its acceptance of God's grace through faith.

   "All these words." They are called "the ten words;" we call them the Decalog. *The first three Commandments tell us about our relationship with God.* Jesus summarizes these Commandments in Matthew 22:37: "Jesus replied: 'Love the Lord your God with all your heart and with all your soul and with all your mind.'"

   The last seven Commandments tell about our relationship with others. Jesus gives a summary of these Commandments in Matthew 22:39: "And the second is like it: 'Love your neighbor as yourself.'"

   Summarize all of the Commandments in one word: _____

2. The first Commandment forbids the adoration of any creature, visible or invisible, or any part of creation. All images and likenesses of God reduce the Creator to creature-likeness. The one, true God is not like any creature in heaven above, on the earth, or under the earth. In the Old Testament "gods" and "idols" are similar words. "Idol" means "good for nothing." Expressly forbidden: spiritism, witchcraft, astrology, and all forms of the occult.

What "other gods" are we tempted to "worship" today? _____

_____

"Jealous." God is not jealous in the human sense, but in the sense that idolatry is an insult to His infinite holiness. To worship any man-made caricature of God is no small sin. Those who do so hate God, and His wrath is upon them.

3. Do "not misuse the name of the Lord." This means to use it in vanity, lying, or any kind of sin. God's name is a revelation of Himself. James writes: "Above all, my brothers, do not swear -- not by heaven or by earth or by anything else. Let your 'Yes' be yes, and your 'No,' no, or you will be condemned" (James 5:12).

Expressions like "O God," "Christ," "Oh, my goodness," "oh, heavens," "By gosh," and so on are also forbidden. We call these apocopated oaths. Apocopate means "cutting off, omission of the last sound or syllable of a word." Jesus says, "But I tell you, Do not swear at all: either by heaven, for it is God's throne; or by the earth, for it is his footstool; or by Jerusalem, for it is the city of the Great King. And do not swear by your head, for you cannot make even one hair white or black" (Matthew 5:34-36).

4. "Remember the Sabbath day by keeping it holy." God's people have always worshiped Him, but not always in a more formal celebration. This command was only for the Jews and served as a discernable mark that they were the Lord's special, holy people. According to Colossians 2:16-17 and other verses we, too, are to worship at a public gathering; the day of the week for such worship, however, is left up to us. True or False: The Third Commandment, as given to Moses on Sinai, is the only Commandment that has been abrogated.

5. In the following Commandments note how the sanctity of parenthood, life, etc., is protected. "Honor your father and your mother, so that you may live long in the land the Lord your God

is giving you." Parents are God's stand-ins, His representatives. To honor parents is to honor God. In Ephesians 6:2-3 Paul calls this the first Commandment with a promised special blessing such as long life.

"You shall not murder." God normally reserves to Himself the right to take life. "You shall not commit adultery." Extramarital sex is forbidden. The penalty is severe: death. "You shall not steal." Everyone's property is to be honored and protected. "You shall not give false testimony against your neighbor." All lying and falsehoods are forbidden. "You shall not covet..." To covet means to desire or long after something that is not yours, but belongs to someone else. This section closes with the fear of God present in the people.

6. Romans 3:20 says, "Therefore no one will be declared righteous in His (God's) sight by observing the law; rather, through the law we become conscious of sin." What purpose of the Law is stated here?

_____

What do we see when we look into the mirror of God's Law?

_____

Why are the first three Commandments called vertical laws?

_____

Why are the last seven Commandments called horizontal laws?

_____

7. In Exodus 21 we read about the Israelite Civil Law. In Exodus 23:14-17 we read about Religious Law. The Ten Commandments are called the Moral Law. Why? _____

_____

8. True or False: Keeping the Commandments will not save us, but they will help us get to heaven. Why? _____
In the second stanza of "Rock of Ages" we confess:

> Not the labors of my hands Can fulfil Thy law's demands;
> Could my zeal no respite know, Could my tears forever flow,
> All for sin could not atone; Thou must save, and Thou alone.

Will keeping the Commandments help us live happier lives here on earth? _____ Why? _____

9. It has been said that the First Commandment is the most important of all the Commandments. Why do you think that is true?

_____

10. True or False: I have sinned against each of the Ten Commandments. For this disobedience God's judgment of eternal death is upon me – nothing to laugh about. However, I have forgiveness for all my sins through Jesus who has died for me upon the cross and who has been obedient to each Commandment for me. If I died today, I would go to heaven. I know this for sure!

Let's Wrap It Up

1. This story teaches me that God _____

_____

2. This story teaches me that Israel _____

_____

3. This story teaches me that I (truths) _____

_____

(actions) _____

Closing Prayer

Closing Hymn

Come, holy Comforter, Your sacred witness bear In this glad hour! Your sev'n fold gifts impart; Rule now in ev'ry heart; Never from us depart, Spirit of pow'r.

To the great One in Three Eternal praises be Hence evermore! Your sov'reign majesty May we in glory see And to eternity Love and adore.

Bible Reading Schedule for the Next Seven Days

❑ 1st day – Exodus 15
❑ 2nd day – Exodus 16
❑ 3rd day – Exodus 17
❑ 4th day – Exodus 18
❑ 5th day – Exodus 19
❑ 6th day – Exodus 20
❑ 7th day – Exodus 21

You have just finished **A Time To Laugh... or Cry** Part 1. Here are the lesson titles for **A Time To Laugh... or Cry** Part 2:

Lesson 11   When Israel Conquered Canaan
Lesson 12   With Gideon, God's Man of Action
Lesson 13   With Samson, Strong and Foolish
Lesson 14   With David, the Soldier Boy and King
Lesson 15   During the Building - Dedication of Solomon's Temple
Lesson 16   At a Daring Contest of the Prophet Elijah
Lesson 17   With Jonah, the Reluctant Evangelist
Lesson 18   At What Isaiah Saw and Said
Lesson 19   With Faithful Daniel and His Friends
Lesson 20   At Malachi's Message of Despair and Hope

You can order Part 2 using the address on page 1.

Heaven. Just the mention of the word boggles our minds and moves our hearts! Going to heaven appeals to us as the greatest adventure possible. Christian parents teach their children about heaven. Sooner or later everyone thinks about heaven, even those who deny it. It has constancy and tremendous appeal. Now there is an exciting seven lesson study based on the very teachings of Holy Scripture on this subject. It's titled: **The Many Wonders of Heaven** with these lesson titles –

Lesson 1   The Wonder of Entrance
Lesson 2   The Wonder of God
Lesson 3   The Wonder of the Saints
Lesson 4   The Wonder of God's Family
Lesson 5   The Wonder of Reward
Lesson 6   The Wonder of Activity
Lesson 7   The Wonder of the City

Ask for a free brochure which describes all of our materials. Our address and phone number are on page 1.